CRUNCH TIME™

CRUNCH TIME™

*Eight Steps to Making
the Right Life Decisions
at the Right Times*

KEN LINDNER

GOTHAM BOOKS

GOTHAM BOOKS
Published by Penguin Group (USA) Inc.
375 Hudson Street, New York, New York 10014, U.S.A.
Penguin Books Ltd, Registered Offices: 80 Strand, London WC2R 0RL, England
Penguin Books Australia Ltd, 250 Camberwell Road, Camberwell, Victoria 3124, Australia
Penguin Books Canada Ltd, 10 Alcorn Avenue, Toronto, Ontario, Canada M4V 3B2
Penguin Books (NZ), cnr Airborne and Rosedale Roads, Albany, Auckland 1310, New Zealand

Published by Gotham Books, a division of Penguin Group (USA) Inc.

First printing, January 2005
10 9 8 7 6 5 4 3 2 1

Grateful acknowledgement is made for permission to reprint the following:

An excerpt from Broadcasting Realities by Ken Lindner, copyright © 1999 Ken Lindner. Reprinted with permission of Bonus Books, Inc.

Gotham Books and the skyscraper logo are trademarks of Penguin Group (USA) Inc.

LIBRARY OF CONGRESS CATALOGING-IN-PUBLICATION DATA
Lindner, Ken.
    Crunch time : eight steps to making the right life decisions at the right times. / by Ken Lindner.
        p. cm.
    ISBN: 1-592-40098-1 (hardcover : alk. paper)
    1. Decision making.   2. Self–actualization (Psychology)   I. Title.
    BF448.L55 2005
    153.8'3—dc22   2004019310

Printed in the United States of America
Set in Galliard
Designed by Heather Saunders

This book is printed on acid-free paper. ♾

ACKNOWLEDGMENTS AND DEDICATIONS

Thank you to:

My parents, Betty and Jack Lindner, and to Shelley and Bill Berman, Jack Hartley, Dr. Charles Masterson, Richard Scheer, Martine Zoller, and Lanie and Joe Havens for filling my *Heart-of-Hearts* with love;

Mel Berger, for believing in me and this book, and for your stellar representation and advice;

Lauren Marino and Bill Shinker, for immediately and enthusiastically embracing *Crunch Time* and making it a reality; Hilary Terrell, for your invaluable help and support;

My clients, for believing in me and entrusting me with your precious careers;

Susan Levin, for running Ken Lindner & Associates (KLA) all these years, and for being such a caring friend; Karen Wang-Lavelle and Kristin Allen, for proofreading my manuscript and sharing their excellent input with me; Shari Freis, for so effectively organizing my life that I was able to write this book; and my other KLA teammates, especially Rick Ramage and Michael Appell, for doing such a great job helping our clients fulfill their potential;

Ben Cammarata, for showing unparalleled loyalty and sensitivity, as well as the foresight to recognize that individuals in their seventies, eighties, and nineties can still make valuable contributions;

Robert Dealy, Robert Morrison, Thomas Dingman, Klaus Freundrich Koch, Sam Weisbord, and Lee Stevens for seeing my abilities and potential. Roberta Lee, for your excellent typing work.

Crunch Time is dedicated to you, Dad, for teaching me how to live, love, and constructively navigate through life, by way of your words and your awesome example; and to you, Mom, for your psychological and sociological insights and wisdom, your love of learning, and your sensitivity to others, which comprise the foundation upon which this book is based. Mom, *Crunch Time* is an embodiment and a reflection of your love, your humaneness, and your brilliance.

CONTENTS

INTRODUCTION

I have devoted my professional and personal lives to enabling people to fulfill their potential, by giving them the tools to make *wise, constructive,* and *self-enhancing* decisions. It gives me incredible satisfaction to see the individuals with whom I've worked and/or coached enhance themselves and others by thinking and acting in constructive ways, so that they not only achieve their most cherished goals, but also develop valid, positive self-esteem in the process. And, as you will glean from what follows, the process or manner in which you reach your decisions is vitally important to your psychological and emotional well-being.

There is no question that one of my good fortunes is that I have been able to identify talented individuals, early in their careers, and secure their representation. However, I have observed over and over again that *talent alone is merely unrealized potential.* Attaining sustained success in any endeavor takes more than just talent, ability, or heartfelt dreams—it requires rock-solid decision-making skills, based upon constructive and self-enhancing *decision-making strategies.*

I was blessed, as a late-blooming child, to have loving parents—especially a mother—who believed in me, effectively counseled me, and never made me feel "less than." As a result of this support, my extensive athletic endeavors, and the creation and implementation of my *Crunch Time Decision-Making Strategies,* I have grown to be much happier and have achieved many of my goals and dreams. Due in large part to this good feeling and success, my life mission is to believe in and counsel others, so that they can achieve their most precious goals and develop legitimate high self-esteem.

In the film *Dead Poets Society,* prep-school teacher John Keating, portrayed by Robin Williams, shares the following thought about life with his students:

The powerful play goes on and you may
contribute a verse. What will that verse be?

What you are about to read in *Crunch Time* is the heart and soul of my life's work and verse. I believe that if you take the time to reflect upon and absorb the material herein, it can and will make a very positive difference in how you write the future verses of your life's play.

CRUNCH TIME™

PART

1

Exploring Your Decision-Making Foundation

INTRODUCTION
(CONTINUED)

DECISIONS AND DECISION-MAKING:
AN OVERVIEW

The keys to attaining your goals, fulfilling your dreams, and achieving inner happiness are:

Making Constructive and Enhancing Decisions and
Thereafter Acting Consistently with These Decisions
for as Long as They Remain Constructive and Enhancing

Every day, we're faced with all sorts of issues, choices, and decisions that affect our lives to varying degrees. Some decisions will change our lives forever. In some cases, just a few critical decisions can make a world of difference in a person's life. Other decisions are less profound, but still have an important impact on whether we eventually achieve our large and small goals. *The act of making constructive decisions and doing positive things for ourselves makes us feel good about ourselves.* This good feeling, in turn, propels and catalyzes us to do more and more enhancing things for ourselves. Conversely, destructive and self-sabotaging decision-making and behavior diminish the quality of our lives and—in our *Heart-of-Hearts*—make us feel bad about ourselves. Therefore, it behooves you to strive to rid yourself of unhealthy decision-making strategies and to develop, modify, and keep the enhancing ones, in order to become the wisest decision-maker you can be and thereby fulfill your positive potential.

You are the result of your decisions! The state of your life and your inner happiness, in large part, are reflections of your decisions. Your decisions are your very precious opportunities—each and every one of them—to either raise the quality of your life and the lives of those around you, or to lower the quality. They are your wonderful chances—your everyday gifts—all there for the taking, to seize your "gold-ring" (forget the brass stuff!) dreams.

There is no question in my mind that what separates those individuals who achieve their goals and realize their most cherished dreams from those who don't is *the process* by which the achievers reach their decisions.

During my twenty years as a career counselor and choreographer, I've worked with scores of individuals who have learned to think through and deal with things constructively. Not surprisingly, a great majority of them have achieved the highest pinnacles of success. Interestingly, a number of these successful people have achieved even more than their natural talent might indicate that they could. (I am one of them.) Their constructive mind-sets and strategies enabled and empowered them to become super- or overachievers. For instance, I would argue that tennis great Chris Evert didn't possess some of the physical strength or natural athletic gifts that some of her competitors enjoyed. She didn't have anything resembling a powerful serve and she rarely came to the net to volley, yet she dominated women's tennis for years. Why? Because she was so mentally and emotionally strong and constructive. On the other hand, I know far too many people who have undermined themselves through their destructive decision-making and thought processes. As a result, time after time, they experience crushing defeats, because without constructive and effective decision-making skills and strategies, even the most brilliant talent can be wasted. Not only do these often supremely gifted individuals never come close to fulfilling their potential, and therefore fail to taste the sweet, high-self-esteem fruits of well-made decisions, but in many instances, they also destroy significant portions of their own lives and the lives of those around them.

Let's take a moment to compare the following words:

Enhancing	vs.	Sabotaging
Fulfilled	vs.	Empty
Constructive	vs.	Destructive
Positive	vs.	Negative
Healthy	vs.	Toxic
Proactive	vs.	Victim
Successful	vs.	Failure

How do *you* want to describe yourself, your decisions, and your decision-making processes?

I'm sure that if you're reading this book, you'd probably choose the left-hand column. Yet as sure as death follows life, we all engage in some amount of diminishing, destructive, and toxic decision-making.

No one in this world is perfect. The key is to become the very best decision-maker you can. My mom once shared the following thought with me: "I'd rather strive for perfection and fall short, then strive for mediocrity and attain it." Smart person, my mom!

Let's strive to be the best we can be. Constructive decision-making can be simple. You just have to *want to learn, want to grow,* and *want to lift the quality of your life.*

WHY DO WE MAKE SUCH BAD DECISIONS?!

Ever since I became a career counselor, I've been stunned by how often bright and talented individuals make self-destructive and self-sabotaging decisions. It's absolutely amazing, and a profoundly sad reality.

I see examples of poisonous decision-making throughout my day.

Witness the fact that so many people: stay in relationships that are diminishing and emotionally and/or psychologically toxic; smoke cigarettes, even though there is clear evidence that smoking is deadly to themselves and to others in the vicinity; take recreational drugs, such as heroin, crack, cocaine, etc., when they *know* that they are risking their health; overeat to an unhealthy extent or to the point of obesity; consume alcohol in dangerous amounts and/or drink and drive; have unprotected sex in this era of AIDS; and, most of all, engage in activities that they, in their *Heart-of-Hearts,* know are destructive and dangerous to the emotional, psychological, and physical well-being of themselves and valued others.

Destructive decision-making and self-sabotage are all around us. For example, is there a more blatant illustration of self-destructive behavior than the Kobe Bryant case? Kobe seemed to have everything going for him. He is a top professional basketball player; he earns millions of dollars a year in salary and more than ten times that in product endorsements; he has a beautiful young wife and a new child; and he was one of the most respected and beloved athletes of our time. For some reason, however, he made a decision that put all this at risk, for what appears to be an hour or so of physical pleasure.

To the general observer, Kobe was "crazy" to have sex with the woman, regardless of consent. But I must tell you, Kobe Bryant is no different from any of us. At times, we all make flawed and self-destructive decisions—especially when our emotions come into play. The difference between Kobe and almost everyone else is that Kobe's destructive decision-making is front and center in the public spotlight, and his humiliation, potential losses, and fall from grace have been, and will be, far more dramatic than most.

What is especially interesting about Kobe is that in some areas of his life, such as his basketball endeavors, he has learned through focused practice and well-thought-out preparation to make excellent reflexive decisions. He knows when and how to dribble the ball past defenders and drive to the basket for a dunk or a layup, when to stop and shoot a jump shot, etc. Through focused practice and preparation, he has attained almost thorough mastery and control of his mental, emotional, and physical skills on the basketball court. However, when certain personal emotions, emotional weaknesses, needs, and/or temptations were involved or triggered—which he had *not* taken the requisite time to prepare to deal with constructively—Kobe, like all of us at one time or another, seemingly reacted thoughtlessly and reflexively by making a devastatingly destructive and self-sabotaging decision. Part of the problem is that when we're faced with important decisions, we often have little or no time to think things through objectively, in order to reach the most constructive short- and long-term decisions.

It has been my experience that the primary key to self-enhancing decision-making is to be mentally, emotionally, and psychologically prepared *when decisions are required.* This is especially true when the situation is triggered by particular emotions, needs, or cravings. Very often, we make bad decisions because we do not prepare ourselves, in advance, to deal with the possible, or probable, opportunities, issues, temptations, etc., that are likely to come our way.

Crunch Time provides you with the thought processes, the skills, and the *Crunch Time Steps* and *Strategies* that will prepare and empower you to make great personal and professional decisions. Equipped with this material, you can change and lift the quality of your life in the most wonderful and self-enhancing way, by making decisions that will enable you to fulfill your positive potential, achieve your dreams, and allow you to feel good—and often great—about yourself. These positive feelings, in turn, will motivate and fuel you to make more and more self-enhancing decisions. Why? Because you'll feel that you're worth it. And you most certainly are.

Just start making some self-enhancing decisions, and see how good you feel about yourself and your ability and power to constructively change and improve the quality of your life.

BEFORE WE BEGIN

At the beginning of our journey together, it's important to recognize and remember that should some of the ensuing material seem familiar or repetitious, don't fret. Many of us have at some time in our lives been to places where for some reason, we've not seen all there was to see or learned all there was to learn. Then again, sometimes seeing familiar things, situations, or individuals from another vantage point, in another context, or at a later time, can often be quite different and illuminating. Actually, it might not be until perhaps the second or third time around that we are truly ready and able to more fully appreciate someone or something for their previously overlooked real qualities and virtues. Therefore, throughout our trip together, we will utilize some familiar material as a reminder—in essence a refresher course—to help you get on, or back on, the right decision-making track.

Throughout my career, I have been exposed to many formulas for personal change and growth that rely upon the Band-Aid approach of simply changing our attitudes and our facades. In today's world of quick fixes and superficial solutions, these theories can appear very attractive. And they may work—when things are going well. But when crises hit, deep conflicts occur, and tough choices need to be made, these matchstick foundations often fall apart, our positive facades fade or crumble, and we tend to revert back to our old, reflexive, ineffective decision-making processes and strategies for dealing with problems. All of our resolve and resolutions go—as Paul Simon sang—"slip sliding away." The reason is: *Formulas that change only facades basically focus upon changing the symptoms of our problems; they don't deal with and eradicate or alleviate their causes.* We can't cure cancer with a spray of Bactine and a nice bandage. Deeper explorations and more intricate procedures and remedies are required.

Additionally, there are many self-help theories that deal exclusively and/or primarily with cerebral/cognitive solutions to behavioral problems. Therefore, they don't sufficiently deal with the all-important emotional aspects of the decision-making equation. As a result, these theories often fall short, because, as we all know, our emotions often override our better judgment. *Crunch Time* focuses on both the *cerebral* and the *emotional* components of decision-making and behavior. The material presented herein acknowledges the awesome influence that our emotions can have on our decision-making. However, through various *anticipatory, preparatory,* and *destructive-emotion nullifying* steps, the powerful force of negative emotions that often lead us to reach self-destructive decisions can be counteracted or vitiated.

If we are to lead healthier, more constructively productive lives, and make them great; if we are to come close to fulfilling our true potential; and if we are to achieve our most cherished and precious goals, we must go to the heart of our problems, and understand them and deal with them. *We must reevaluate and rebuild our decision-making foundations and processes, and solidly reinforce them with the "internal goods" that will actually allow us to attain our goals and fulfill our dreams, and continue to enjoy them over time.*

The means by which we can take constructive ownership of our lives lies in how we reach our decisions.

Daniel Goleman, in his popular book *Emotional Intelligence,* writes that individuals with a high intelligence quotient (IQ), aren't always the most successful navigators of real-life situations, because some of them seemingly lack the emotional intelligence of other more emotionally developed and streetwise individuals. *Crunch Time* takes Mr. Goleman's book a step or two further, explaining and illustrating how you can become more emotionally intelligent (and, as a result, more self-fulfilled), by learning to make wiser, more constructive, and more self-enhancing decisions. In essence, the material in this book will equip you with the decision-making skills and *Strategies* that will help you to fulfill your great potential. The explanation is simple: If you can make constructive and self-enhancing decisions time after time, you put yourself in the best position to achieve your goals and fulfill your dreams.

Crunch Time is divided into three sections. The first identifies and discusses decision-making terms and concepts. These are the essential mental, psychological, and emotional building blocks that form the foundation for making constructive and self-enhancing decisions.

Section two is an in-depth study of *"The Eight Crunch Time Steps"* for making constructive decisions. This section also presents the *"Crunch Time Decision-Making Strategies"* (hereafter referred to as either *"Crunch Time Strategies"* or *"Strategies"*), as well as *Strategy* bullet-points called

"Strata-Gems." These *Strategies* and *Strata-Gems* have, with great consistency and efficacy, led me and my clients to make enhancing and success-evoking decisions.

Throughout *Crunch Time*, there are stories involving my clients to help you more fully visualize and absorb the points presented in each chapter.

Ready to begin feeling *great* about yourself and your decisions?

Let's get started . . .

EXPLORING YOUR DECISION-MAKING FOUNDATION

THE CONCEPT OF *CRUNCH TIME*

One of the great benefits that I derived from being an athlete and studying different sports is that I learned to identify *Crunch Time*, and thereafter developed the ability to, in many instances, respond constructively when a *Crunch Time* challenge is presented to me.

The other day, the news manager of a television station called me about my client, Terry. He said that he would be giving Terry a plum assignment that afternoon that would showcase Terry's broadcasting strengths. This manager told me that Terry was one of three people who were being considered for a coveted national position, and that if my client was on his game and really showed his stuff, he would likely get the position. The manager finished our conversation by saying, "Kenny, I can't be any clearer than this: If Terry gets it right, his career is changed for the better from here on out. It's up to him. Starting this afternoon, *it's Crunch Time!*"

The last few minutes of a close game are sometimes referred to as *Crunch Time*—a critical point during a sports contest in which the outcome of the game can go either way. *Crunch Times* are those pivotal points and defining moments when individuals are faced with significant choices. They are our opportunities to either make wise decisions and enhance ourselves and others, or to make poor and diminishing decisions, which often result in our being destructive to ourselves and to others.

As someone who counsels individuals every day regarding their making the most positive and healthy career and life decisions possible, I have found the concept of *Crunch Time* to be a particularly useful, effective, and visual one.

I believe that not enough attention is paid to the fact that each of us faces *Crunch Times*—or moments of decision—many times each day throughout our lives. For example, we often must decide whether or not we will eat or drink something that will cause us to gain weight or affect us negatively in some other way; whether or not we will light up a cigarette or cigar; whether or not we will remain in a personal or professional relationship that we know isn't healthy for us, etc.

Crunch Times are those instances when individuals who are committed to excellence (star performers) often step up to positively and effectively meet the challenges before them. They combine presence of mind with *knowledge, understanding,* and *educated and prepared instinct* to correctly analyze the situation of the moment. These individuals then adapt their performances to make the maximum use of their analyses (by making the right and/or best choices), thereby raising the level of their games to attain a successful outcome. They turn great potential into positive reality.

This ability isn't acquired overnight. It requires focused thought, analysis, preparation, and practice, along with great desire, enthusiasm, and tenacious persistence to achieve the sought-after goals. A *proactive approach* and *appropriate discipline* are also critical components of optimal performance at *Crunch Time*. One *Crunch Time* quality that makes all of the others viable and effective is an accurate understanding of the situation at hand and of the elements and individuals involved. True understanding of the pivotal elements that comprise a constructive decision is the foundation upon which all *Crunch Time* qualities are based.

"Behaviorism"—A Quick Look Back

It was during my first college psychology class that I was introduced to the works of Ivan Pavlov, B. F. Skinner, and other behavioral theorists. Do you remember the dog in Pavlov's stimulus/response experiment? During the initial stage of that experiment, a bell would sound and a dog would immediately be fed some meat. With the repetition of this ringing and feeding scenario, as soon as the dog heard the bell, it would salivate, expecting that it would be fed. With further repetition, the dog began to *reflexively* salivate upon hearing the bell—even without the meat being present, which had been the initial stimulus for the salivation. In essence, when presented with a familiar situation—hearing the bell—Pavlov's pooch reflexively and non-discerningly reacted with a behavioral pattern of response—and strategy—that it perceived had worked in the past.

Other scientists took Pavlov's findings further, by theorizing that individuals seek out pleasurable experiences and avoid painful ones. Based upon those premises, they asserted that individuals' actions can be *conditioned* and *reinforced*, based upon the introduction of positive and negative stimuli.

While maximizing the importance of positive and negative reinforcement and their impact upon molding behavior, these theorists often minimized some of the most valuable qualities of a human being: The abilities to consciously think, analyze, reason, reflect, prepare, and choose to make value-based decisions.

Popular authors such as M. Scott Peck and Stephen Covey have pointed out that there can and should be a step between the introduction of a stimulus or event and a person's response to it. Dr. Peck writes that this period separating stimulus from response is a time to "bracket," or hold in abeyance, our old responses and/or behavioral patterns, and to decide whether the situation at hand calls for a new behavioral pattern, a modification of the old one, or the usual response.

It is the intervening step—or period of time—between when a stimulus or situation is presented to us and when we choose to act (constructively or destructively) that we will refer to as *Crunch Time*.

Crunch Times are those precious moments when we *can act* (as opposed to *reflexively react*), and *consciously decide* to raise the quality of our personal and professional lives, or we can *compulsively react*, often non-discerningly reenacting our old, inappropriate behavioral strategies, and thus diminish the quality of our lives in one way or another.

It's your goal on our journey together and throughout the rest of your life to become the best *Crunch Time* performer and decision-maker you can be.

Strata-Gems:

- *Crunch Times* are those instances when you are faced with important decisions. They are *opportunities* for you to either enhance or diminish your life. The key is to *seize the moment* and make a *great* decision.
- At *Crunch Time*, you want to *think through* and *consciously choose* your actions.

THE "CRUNCH TIME CONTINUUM": UNDERSTANDING THE TIMING OF YOUR DECISIONS

In your quest to understand and master decision-making, it is important that you picture in your mind's eye the three times when you most often make your decisions. These times are reflected in *The Crunch Time Continuum*.

The Crunch Time Continuum

Pre–Crunch Time Decisions   *Crunch Time Decisions*   *Post–Crunch Time Decisions*

Throughout the rest of this book, we will examine decisions and the times at which we make them. Let's define them:

- *Crunch Time Decisions*: These occur when a situation is presented to you, and within a short period thereafter, you must decide what to do. Some examples are:
  A. *The Situation*: You are offered a piece of birthday cake at a party.
     The Issue: Do you eat it?
  B. *The Situation*: Someone says something to you that you interpret as being critical of you.
     The Issue: How do you respond to the criticism?
  C. *The Situation*: You find that your fourteen-year-old son/daughter has been hiding something from you that greatly disturbs you (he/she has been smoking, skipping class, etc.).
     The Issue: What do you do about it?

- *Pre–Crunch Time Decisions*: These decisions are made minutes, hours, days, or months *before* you are presented with the actual stimulus or situation that will trigger your decision. These decisions are reached in anticipation of choices that will or may have to be made at a later time. Some examples of *Pre-Crunch Time Decisions* are:
  A. When you're offered a piece of birthday cake tonight at the party, no matter how tempted you are, you decide that you won't eat it.
  B. When Sheila/Sam brings up the same complaint that you're not attentive enough to her/him anymore, you're going to tell her/him how you truly feel about her/his demands on your time.
  C. From now on, when your mom/dad/boss/client drives you crazy or pushes one of your buttons, you're not

going to react in anger. Instead, you decide that you're going to calmly and coolly step away from the situation, think about it, and choose an appropriate response. It's your New Year's resolution.

- *Post–Crunch Time Decisions*: These decisions are made moments, hours, days, or months after you have made your original decision. They are decisions that reflect whether you want to (a) continue the behavior that resulted from your prior decision, (b) do the opposite of it, or (c) modify it. Some examples are:
  A. Prior to Thanksgiving, you decided that you would stick to your new diet throughout the holiday season; and indeed, you did it. As a result, you look and feel great! You assess the situation and decide that you're going to continue to practice discipline and intelligent judgment from now on when it comes to eating.

  In this instance, you choose to stay the course.
  B. You decided to give it all up and move to Los Angeles to become an actress/actor. After months of trying to find a reputable agent to represent you, you settled for anyone who will send you out on auditions. During the next six months, you went on three cattle-call auditions and didn't get call-backs for any of them. You feel empty, disoriented, and demoralized by show business and a city that seems to lack roots, a soul, and humanity. You assess your prior decision, and conclude that this lifestyle is unhealthy. You decide: "I've done it. I've had it. I'm going back to my friends, my family, and my advertising job in Chicago."

  In this case, you choose to change the course of your original decision and your behavior.
  C. For the past fifteen years, you've worked six days a week and about sixteen hours a day. You assess this decision and conclude that there *must* be more to life

than just working. You're now a partner in your firm and you're more than comfortable financially, but you're not happy—enough. You decide to adjust your behavior by: working five days a week—and sometimes four; taking all of your vacation time; leaving work at reasonable hours; and making your leisure time and your enjoyment of life higher priorities.

In this instance, you decide to modify your old decision.

As we continue our journey, it's important to keep *The Crunch Time Continuum* and the timing of your decisions in mind.

THE CONCEPT OF *MASTERY*

An essential element of your emotional health and the fulfillment of your goals and dreams is your development of the mind-set and skill of *mastery*. That is, the attempted performance of an act, followed by its successful completion. The mastering of an act may require you to perform some or all of the following functions:

1) *Identifying a goal* that you want to attain;
2) *Thinking about the goal* and a preferred means of attaining it;
3) *Devising a plan* of action;
4) *Visualizing* the overall sequence of events involved in goal attainment;
5) *Preparing* to effectuate the plan;
6) *Effectuating* the plan of action;
7) Satisfactorily *completing* the plan and attaining the goal;
8) *Acknowledging* and *cognitively celebrating the successful completion* of the plan of action and goal attainment.

Exploring Mastery

There are few goals that appear unattainable to someone who has had positive mastery experiences. For example, golf phenomenon Tiger Woods made history by winning his third U.S. Junior Amateur golf title. As he reflected upon his victorious final round, which began with him trailing his opponent by five strokes, he was quoted as saying: "I knew what I had to do. I'd done it [come back and won after trailing by many strokes] before."

Conversely, through my experiences, I have found that *you never truly know that you can do something until you've actually done it.* For instance, I had a friend, years ago, whose parents were extremely wealthy. They gave him everything, and everything was done *for* him. Nothing was done *by* him. We were both eighteen at the time, when I noticed that he had no core confidence, as he never truly knew what he could accomplish. He could guess. He could hope. But in his *Heart-of-Hearts*, he didn't know. He began to stutter. He didn't get along with other kids. He had an inner anger.

My friend was monetarily wealthy—yet he was one of the most deprived and impoverished individuals I had ever met. His parents crippled him by not allowing him to take steps on his own, to occasionally stumble and fall, and to eventually accomplish the goals of walking and running by himself. To this day, he is foundering. He has no core confidence in his ability to meet a challenge. This is because he has never developed the skill of mastering his decisions or his actions.

A similar story was recently told to me. A forty-five-year-old woman had been born into a very wealthy family. She never held a job in her life. Her daughter confided that for years her mother had longed to have some kind of job, just so that she could know and feel that she could actually accomplish something. Then, about three years ago, a restaurateur was visiting the mother's house, and like many others before him, he noted how beautifully she had decorated it. At the end of the afternoon, he inquired as to whether her mother would be interested (for a fee, of course) in decorating his restaurant for its grand opening. She replied that she would be thrilled to do it. They agreed that work would begin three days later.

During the intervening days, the woman, at different times, appeared scared, distraught, and distant. She showed no signs of excitement or anticipation about beginning her first real job.

Ultimately, the woman never showed up to work on the restaurant and never returned any of the restaurateur's calls. According to her daughter, her mother was so deathly afraid to fail that she never attempted to do the job. And to this day, the woman has *never* worked. She just goes flitting and partying through life.

You may have heard the proverb: "*Give* me a fish, and I can eat for a day. *Teach* me to fish, and I can eat for a lifetime." My spin on this proverb is: "If you do tasks for me, or if I passively let fate decide what will happen to me, I will just rely on others and/or other forces to determine my life. But if I learn to *proactively master* and take control of my decisions and my acts, and I consistently do these things, I become self-reliant. I put myself in the best position to *positively determine* my own fate. I thus take ownership of my life."

Time and time again, I have seen individuals accomplish their goals and rise above their backgrounds and the pack, because in their *Heart-of-Hearts* they believe, "If I have any talent in an area, I have the cerebral and emotional mastery strategies to accomplish my goals. Since I've done it before, I know I can do it again."

When individuals know and feel that they have the capability to identify a desired goal, to visualize, implement, and complete a plan of action, and to ultimately attain that goal, the feeling of empowerment is huge. The positive self-esteem that is generated is clearly earned and thus valid. This inner knowledge and feeling are basic and enduring major elements of a rock-solid foundation of great decision-making and high self-esteem.

Understanding and attaining mastery of positive and enhancing behaviors, skills, and goals is a cornerstone of consistently making and implementing great decisions. Being masterful is an incredibly empowering ability.

THE CONCEPTS OF UNDERSTANDING
AND OWNERSHIP

Years ago, a story was told to me about a reporter who was assigned by his TV station to cover a serious accident. The story allegedly unfolded this way:

Upon arriving at the scene of the accident, the reporter quickly and without great care scanned the area. He then went on to do some other things—such as watch a baseball playoff game on TV—until it was time to deliver his report. As the reporter began his presentation, he did his trademark "walk and talk" routine, walking around the accident scene and directing the camera to various points of interest while he flawlessly delivered the facts that he had memorized earlier.

When the reporter finished, the studio anchor advised both the reporter and the viewers that an unexpected development had just occurred. The anchor shared the development with the reporter and the viewers, and then asked the reporter to "analyze how the information might affect the situation." Upon hearing the question, the reporter immediately panicked. His brain apparently locked, and he couldn't speak for what seemed like an excruciatingly endless amount of time. As the reporter had only surveyed the surface facts about the story, he didn't understand its essentials, and therefore, he had no clue as to how to intelligently respond to the ever-changing situation. A moment or so later, the anchor nervously asked the question again. The reporter continued to stand there, speechless, staring blankly into the camera. Finally, the reporter began to speak. However, to everyone's embarrassment, he began to simply regurgitate the memorized facts, word for word, that he had given moments earlier—while never attempting to answer the anchor's question. As he did this, a near-hysterical producer implored the anchor to segue, as soon as possible, out of the report and back to the studio.

The reporter was fired soon thereafter.

On the other end of the spectrum, there are reporters who pride themselves on attaining a thorough understanding of their material. They can deliver their stories during torrential downpours, amidst gunfire, in the face of gale-force winds, and with curve after unexpected curve being thrown at them. And through it all, they don't lose their presence of mind or their ability to creatively and effectively deal with and thrive when major changes or delicate nuances are presented. By familiarizing themselves with and understanding the elements of their story, they can see everything in the insightful context of the *"Big Picture."* These individuals are said to have taken ownership of their work. They've mastered the material and made it their own.

Having been in the representation business for twenty years and a *Student of Life* for even longer, I see examples of both ends of the spectrum every day. Some individuals take responsibility for, and master their actions and decisions in a healthy and proactive manner. Others, passively and/or destructively, do not.

We are all *performers* in life in that day in and day out we perform hundreds of functions. The reporter who froze was a performer who didn't understand the why and the how of the story that he was reporting on. He only knew the superficial facts, and he didn't care enough to have a deeper understanding of the situation. Therefore, during a crisis period, when others with a more thorough knowledge and understanding might well have insightfully and adeptly processed and then appropriately responded to the anchor's question, this reporter was unprepared. He froze. He didn't know what to do or say, and he eventually ran for cover to his old (behavioral) script—literally!

In life, many of us act as this reporter did, by taking the path of least resistance. We perform the familiar scripts of our lives, without any thoughtful preparation, exploration, evaluation, understanding, or ownership. And in crises, we reflexively revert back to, run under the seemingly protective umbrella of, and act out our old behavioral patterns and strategies, even if they are crippling and diminishing and are truly hurting us and preventing our constructive growth.

The day that my life changed immeasurably for the better was the day that I began to take ownership of my decisions and my actions. This ownership required, first and foremost, that I seek to attain a truer and more comprehensive view and understanding of myself and of my behavior, as well as a fuller understanding of others and of the events around me.

Similarly, if you are to make constructive and enhancing decisions that will lead to the attainment of your most cherished goals and your truest inner happiness, you, too, must begin to take ownership of your decisions, of your actions, and of your life.

Strata-Gems:

- In order to positively change your life, you must take *ownership* of your decisions and your life. In order to accomplish this, you must attain a truer understanding of yourself, of relevant others, and of the relevant facts and events around you.

- It's never too late to learn how to take ownership of your decisions and your actions.

STRATEGY AND ITS EXECUTION

As soon as I took up paddle tennis, I learned how important it is to have various effective strategies available to me. A strategy to make time to practice and play. A strategy to keep improving. A strategy for playing a particular opponent. A strategy to get better players to want to include me in their games. A strategy as to how to lose weight, become more agile, gain speed, etc.

Athletics have taught me to *anticipate* and to make *plans*, in advance, that will help me effectively pursue and attain my goals. When strategies worked for me, I learned to integrate them into my decision-making and behavioral repertoires. When they didn't work, I learned to modify or discard them. As I became more mature, I learned that some strategies work in some circumstances but not in others, which means their effectiveness is *context-related*. As I continued to grow, I discovered that you can transfer a strategy from one facet of your life and apply it to another. For example, I used all of my *Strategies* regarding discipline, delayed gratification, mastering each step, *Big-Picture* thinking, etc., that I had successfully employed in my athletic endeavors, to doing my college course-work, starting my businesses, and writing my books.

Athletics have taught me that you must have short-term strategies and long-term strategies, and that you must keep creating, acquiring and adjusting your strategies with each new experience.

Being *constructively strategy-minded* has enabled me and many of my clients to achieve our most cherished dreams.

However, it is crucial to keep in mind that you can be the best strategist, but if you can't effectively execute and implement your strategies at the appropriate time, or in the appropriate place, it can all be for nothing.

The key is to be both a constructive and wise strategist, and to prepare thoroughly, so that you will have the ability to correctly and effectively execute your strategies at *Crunch Time*.

THE CONCEPT OF CARPE DIEM!

Carpe Diem (car-pay dee-um) is Latin for "seize the day"—that is, to make the very most of the moment at hand. The concept of carpe diem is infused with positive and constructive spirit and emotion.

Strata-Gem:

An essential element of being the best decision-maker possible is to become a wise, constructive, and anticipatory strategist.

Throughout our journey, carpe diem will represent your great potential for proactively taking constructive and enhancing ownership of your decisions and your life. The high value we place on this passionate spirit and your precious potential is the foundation upon which every step of our journey is based.

All right! We've just laid the basis of our *decision-making foundation*. On to the fun stuff. . . .

The Eight *Crunch Time Steps that Lead to Healthy and Constructive Decisions That You Can Enjoy Throughout Your Lifetime*

Step 1: *Identify* that a stimulus or situation has been presented or could be presented to you, that calls for you to make a decision now or sometime in the future.

Step 2: *State* what the issue is.

Step 3: *Identify, explore*, and *apply* the appropriate *Crunch Time Strategies* and *Strata-Gems* to the decision before you.

Step 4: *Examine* and *weigh* the relative importance to you of the values involved in your decision.

Step 5: Explore how your decision will affect your *Heart-of-Hearts*.

Step 6: *Frame* the issue before you.

Step 7: Make a *great* decision.

Step 8: *Applaud, celebrate*, and *savor* your constructive decisions, and *review, evaluate, rework, and keep constructive and enhancing decision-making strategies*.

Step 1

IDENTIFY THE SITUATION THAT CALLS FOR YOU TO MAKE A DECISION

This means that you must identify that a situation has been presented, is being presented, will be presented, or could be presented that calls for you to make a decision now, or will call for you to make a decision sometime in the future. Every day, we are presented with stimuli such as events, thoughts, ideas, fears, concerns, etc. These stimuli, in turn, present us with issues (i.e., questions, problems, etc.), about which decisions and choices will have to be made. (See Table 1.)

These stimuli can, for example, be introduced to us by an individual, or by an event that is taking place, has taken place, or will take place sometime in the future. Or, we can initiate and introduce the stimulus ourselves. (See Table 2.)

Table 1

Example of General Stimulus Presented	Example of Specific Stimulus Presented	Example of Issue or Problem to Be Resolved
An "event"	A married couple having sex on their first anniversary.	Is tonight the right time to try to start a family?
A "thought"	"I'm not happy in my job."	Do I want to switch careers?
An "idea"	"I want to do something special for my mom this year."	Do I want to throw her a surprise party and invite all of her friends and family?
A "fear" or "concern"	"Bob/Beth and I just don't communicate anymore."	Do I bring this problem up, and, if so, how and when?

Table 2: Stimulus Introduction

Example of Where the Stimulus Can Come From	*Example of the Stimulus*	*Example of Issue or Problem to be Resolved*
Another individual	Your best friend, Arthur, builds a tennis court in his backyard.	Do I want to start playing tennis again?
An event that is currently taking place	The O.J. Simpson civil verdict is being handed down.	Do I also want to tape the basketball game and the President's State of the Union Address, which are going on at the same time?
An event that will take place	I will be offered a piece of the birthday cake at the party tonight.	Do I stay on my diet and not eat any cake, or is this the time and the place to temporarily go off my diet?
We initiate the stimulus	My friends and I decide to go to Club Med.	What activities will I partake in and when?

Once again, *Step 1,* in this instance, is to identify that a situation or issue has been presented, is being presented, or will be presented that will call for you to make some choice or decision now or in the future.

Step 2
STATE WHAT THE ISSUE IS

This *Step* is fairly self-explanatory. As clearly and concisely as possible, lay out what the *issue* is that needs to be decided. For example:

- Do I eat the piece of pumpkin pie that I'm being offered?

- Do I go to Las Vegas this weekend with my friends, knowing that I have a gambling problem?

- Do I *really* want to go to law school next semester?

- How do I ask my son/daughter about their grades slipping this year?

- Do I have drinks at dinner tonight, when I know that Brent/Susan can't stop drinking once he/she starts?

PART
2

The Crunch Time Strategies

Step 3

IDENTIFY, EXPLORE, AND THEN APPLY THE APPROPRIATE *CRUNCH TIME STRATEGIES*

Once you *actively identify* and *clearly state* the issue that you're dealing with, the next step is to identify, explore, and decide which *Crunch Time Strategies* and which of the healthy and constructive decision-making strategies that you've devised will most effectively help you to reach an enhancing, success-evoking resolution.

What follows are the *Crunch Time Strategies* and *Strata-Gems* that have helped me and my clients reach constructive and self-enhancing decisions. These *Strategies* and *Strata-Gems* are your constructive decision-making guides and formulas. If appropriately and effectively incorporated into your decision-making process, they are sure to help you to become a wiser, and a much more emotionally intelligent and success-evoking decision-maker.

CONSTRUCTIVELY ACTING
—NOT REACTING—
WHEN FACED WITH A DECISION

One of the basic and most important *Strategies* that you can learn is to *act,* consistently, with forethought—and not automatically react—when a situation or stimulus is presented that calls for you to make a decision. Unlike the dog in Pavlov's experiment, instead of succumbing to any initial urges or reflex reactions, you must take the time to *think, explore, evaluate*, and then *honestly choose* your most constructive, efficacious, and enhancing course of action.

A quick story. When I was a high school freshman, our tennis team played a match against one of the strongest high school teams on the East Coast. I played their highly ranked top singles player. By his reputation, I figured that he was probably the best tennis player that I would compete against that year. We played on his team's home courts, and by the time the match began, our court was surrounded with his cheering supporters.

My opponent had never seen me play before. He probably expected an easy match, as our school had never been known for having any strong tennis players. I'm sure that I surprised him by jumping off to a 5-3 lead in the first set. During the next game, he called one of my forehands out that was *clearly* in. When I questioned him on it, he gave me a condescending look and said, "The ball was *out*." He won the game. The next game, with me serving for the set at 5-4, he called a serve of mine out that was really an ace. I became visibly angry, and he knew it. Then, after every point that he won, he yelled, "Point, Mike

Smith." I totally *lost it*. I also lost my composure, my concentration . . . and the match, 7-5, 6-1.

As we walked off the court, my opponent looked at me as if he were my best friend, and said, in what I later learned was his usual condescending way, "You played *so* well. Nice try." In the background, his schoolmates were cheering and giving each other high fives.

After the match, I went to a deserted area, fighting to hold back my tears. Part of me cried. Another part of me wanted to break every racket I had. The intensity of my mixed emotions was as strong as it could be. Up to that point, I had been winning and playing great. He cheated on at least three points, at crucial times, in the first set. Then he did everything he could to distract me. And I reacted just as he wanted me to. I hated him. But I hated myself more, for how stupidly (and destructively) I handled the situation. I hated my emotional weakness.

Interestingly, a few weeks later, on a rainy Sunday afternoon, I was watching a National Basketball Association playoff game. It was a pivotal game for the New York Knicks, who had a chance to become the NBA champions. It was late in the fourth quarter and the score was tied. (*Crunch Time!*) Walt Frazier, the guard who set the tempo for the Knicks, had already scored a slew of clutch baskets, and was single-handedly keeping his team in the game. With a couple of minutes to go, Frazier scored again to put the Knicks in the lead. As the play went to the other side of the court, when no one was looking, one of the opposing players viciously rapped Frazier on the back of the head and brought him to his knees. However, Frazier didn't lose his composure or his concentration. Nor did he try to retaliate in kind, and thus risk being thrown out of that crucial game. Instead, he calmly picked himself up, kept his focus, ran right by his assailant, and a moment later, scored the final and *winning* basket. The sweetest outcome of all!

Upon reflection, I believe that Frazier had said to himself after he was hit: "What do I do? Do I go after the player who hit me and maybe get myself ejected? Or do I focus, and win the series?" I felt that Frazier constructively chose his course of action, based upon what he valued most—winning the NBA title with the Knicks.

I learned a great lesson that day: to appreciate the value of self-control, and to calmly and thoughtfully choose my responses to stimuli, based upon my true values and my most cherished goals. I had let my tennis match against Mike Smith slip away from me, because I had let his distracting tactics and the antics of the spectators influence my playing and thinking. I had reacted reflexively, like Pavlov's dog.

It was on that day that I wrote and developed one of my most important and constructive *Strategies*:

No matter how intense the pressure or how loud the noise,
I'll make sure that I think clearly, and never lose my poise.

(I'm truly thankful that it rained that Sunday, or else I never would have been at home watching the Knicks game. This is but one among an abundance of examples of why I believe that there are no coincidences, and that things often happen for a reason.) The following spring we played Mike Smith's school again. For the second year in a row, the match was to be played on his team's home courts. Lousy scheduling—but I looked forward to it, anyway. This time, I was mentally and emotionally prepared. I knew how I would act—no matter what he tried. (I used some *Pre-Crunch Time* decision-making here.)

We began the match, and I jumped ahead, again. On a crucial point, he cheated, *again*. Even many of the spectators saw it. I took a deep breath. I thought of Walt Frazier. I tuned out all of the cheering and remarks. With me leading 5-4 in the first set, my opponent began to pull the same stuff as the year before, by calling out his name every time he won a point. I won the game and the first set. He became more obnoxious. I became more oblivious to his antics. This, in turn, seemed to throw him more. I focused and won the second set, 6-3, and the match. My preparation had paid off!

Few things in life seemed as sweet. Thanks, Walt.

I cannot overemphasize the crucial importance of proactively preparing constructive and *self-enhancing responses to situations or challenges that can potentially play upon your emotions or emotional weaknesses.*

As I will discuss later, being preparatory and anticipatory has helped client after client achieve wonderful decision-making results.

From experiences such as my two matches with Mike Smith, I developed "The Seven Cs of Non-Reactive Decision-Making," and they have continually served me and my clients well. They are:

1) Stay **C**ool.
2) Think **C**learly.
3) Remain **C**ognizant of the Goal You Want to Attain.
4) Identify **C**onstructive and Positive Means of Goal Attainment.
5) **C**haracter **C**ounts in the decision-making process, because if you feel good about your decision, you'll feel good about who you are. This raises self-esteem.
6) **C**hoose Your Very Best Course of Action.

One other *Strategy* that came out of my first match with Mike Smith is: *Don't let someone else's bad behavior and/or flawed decision-making lead* you *to decide to behave self-destructively.* In our first encounter, I allowed my opponent's antics to make me lose concentration, perspective, and ultimately, the match. Similarly, I have had a number of clients who have let coworkers and managers incite them into making bad behavioral decisions.

For example, about ten years ago, a normally low-key anchor allowed himself, his reputation, and his stature at his station to be dragged through the mud by getting into a savage argument with his often contentious coanchor. Apparently, their mid-newsroom screaming match became so vile that *both* individuals were eventually asked to leave the station . . . permanently.

My client's flawed decision to be sucked into the abusive confrontation was clearly self-destructive. It set his career back for years thereafter.

Strata-Gems:

- Taking time to carefully consider and wisely choose the best course of action—instead of just reacting—is a key *Crunch Time Strategy* . . . and very constructive behavior.

- "No matter how intense the pressure, or how loud the noise, make sure that you think clearly, and never lose your poise."

- Don't let someone else's poor behavior trigger self-destructive decision-making and behavior on your part.

BREAKING AWAY FROM OLD INAPPROPRIATE STRATEGIES— UNDERSTANDING THE DIFFERENCES BETWEEN SIMILAR SITUATIONS

When I was about twenty-three, I was set up on a blind date with a twenty-one-year-old named Melanie. Melanie was smart, great company and, in my view, beautiful. I liked everything about her. During our first summer together, I took her to play tennis, to long dinners filled with great conversation, to movies, and to a couple of Broadway plays. She introduced me to ballet and to such intriguing psychological subjects as music therapy, which she was then studying. Although we had great chemistry, due to the intense pressure that her mom had exerted on her not to have premarital sex, we never consummated the relationship. I cared so much for Melanie and for our relationship—both present and future—that no matter how attracted I was to her (and no matter how strong the sexual urge was at times), I didn't want to push her into doing something she'd regret.

We dated for about a year and a half, although we often didn't see each other a great deal during our college semesters, as we attended schools in different states. However, we kept in touch by phone and mail regularly, until one February day during my senior year in college. That weekend, I was playing in the Princeton Invitational Doubles Championship. I made it all the way to the finals, and I was incredibly excited and wanted to share the news with Melanie. That night I called her at about 10:00 P.M., and then at midnight. No answer. In between calls, I dozed off, trying to rest for the next day's match. I called again, at 3:00 A.M. Still no one home. I didn't know whether to be worried, concerned, or whatever. I decided to put the matter aside as best I could until after the finals. It would be horrible if everything with Melanie were all right and I let a non-problem distract me from winning my match the next day. Besides, my worrying and consternation were not going to benefit anyone. They were nonconstructive acts.

The *Strategy* of not letting a (possible) scenario that I have no control over, or that I don't have any true knowledge about, distract or deter me from attaining my goal has turned out to be a very constructive and enhancing one for me. It helps me to keep my eye on the ball, and thereby perform at my best. For example, despite how much I cared for Melanie, I was able to win the prestigious national title the next day. This *Strategy* also allows me to not expend needless energy being concerned or worried about an event that in the end may never come to pass, or that I can't positively change anyway.

It wasn't until some phone calls and a few angst-ridden days later that I finally caught Melanie at home. As soon as I heard her voice, I knew that something was terribly wrong. All she said was that she had been "dealing with problems," and that she needed to "get away" for a couple of days. She was distant and almost seemed angry. The conversation was painfully short.

I later found out that the night before my tournament finals, Melanie had allegedly gone to a school party, proceeded to drink too much liquor, and had gone home with "some guy," as she described it to a friend, to have non-intimate, unfulfilling sex with him. She felt nothing during the experience, and felt emptiness and guilt after it. She thereafter became intent on proving to herself that "it has to be better than this." So she continued to sleep with the guy, hoping that the sex would feel and be better, and her relationship with him would become more meaningful. She could then feel better about the whole (first) experience. Unfortunately, it never got better and she never felt better.

The incident quickly destroyed our relationship. From then on, Melanie could barely talk to me, and when she did, she became enraged, as she blamed me for her having gotten drunk and having empty sex with just anyone, in order to find out what it was truly like.

I was emotionally blown away by the incident. I truly loved Melanie in every way, and she may well have been a soul mate.

Thereafter, for years, whenever I felt that someone might possibly be betraying me, or not valuing me or our relationship enough, I would either get angry and blow the relationship up—before the other party did or could—or I'd simply bail out of it and withdraw, before risking getting hurt any further. After Melanie and a few other relationship disappointments, I became used to playing the "victim" and came to expect the worst. I reacted routinely and behaved accordingly.

But then there was the Deborah experience. I was dating Deborah for about four months. We seemed to be connecting on all cylinders: cerebrally, romantically, spiritually, etc. She was exceedingly smart, great fun to be with, and beautiful. We had mutual respect for each other and I believed that she had great character. Unfortunately, Deborah and I lived on opposite ends of the country. However, we spoke just about every night.

Then came the Wednesday night she went to a party with a friend. I called a couple of times, including once at 1:00 A.M., but no one answered. Memories of Melanie began to well up within me. The victim mentality of *I'm cruisin' for a bruisin'* began to surface. On the other hand, I was definitely concerned. I *knew* that Deborah wouldn't stay out so late on a weeknight, because she had to be at work early the following morning.

By 11:00 A.M. the next day, I hadn't heard from her. I phoned her office and someone said that Deborah had called in earlier that morning and said that she'd be in that afternoon. Feelings and fears of being the victim, and of again losing someone whom I cared for deeply began to seep into my heart and dance in my head.

However, in this instance, I decided not to react and follow my usual victim decision-making mentality, as I had done for so long. I would instead step away from the uncertainty and angst of the moment to look at how this situation fit into the *"Big Picture"* of my personal relationships. As I examined my track record over the past years, there emerged a constant, unhealthy pattern of behavior, which was: When something in my romantic relationships appeared to go awry or didn't go the way that I expected or wanted it to, I immediately felt bad and expected the worst. I then based my actions upon these hurt feelings and unfulfilled expectations. In my mind, I always heard the tape of my mom telling me that, "If someone you're dating doesn't act or treat you as if she values you, she may *like* you, but she may not like you *enough* (to get serious with her and to expect that she will ultimately treat you as you want to be treated)." In essence, if I expected too much from that person—or I expected her to *act* as if she liked me as much as I liked her—I'd knowingly be cruisin' for a heartbreakin' bruisin'. So, with my mom's perspective in my mind, if someone didn't act as if they valued me enough, I'd blow them off, without ever trying to objectively understand where they were coming from (their subjective perspective of things).

Upon reviewing my past defensive and subjective behavior, I decided to objectively examine my relationship with Deborah, once again, in the context of the *Big Picture*. When I did, I concluded that all of my experiences with her and my perceptions of her up to that point indicated that it was appropriate to trust Deborah, and that she deserved my trust.

I knew that at some point that day I would speak with Deborah. I resolved that I wouldn't play the victim, be accusatory, or appear in any way as if I didn't trust her, as I had in prior situations with other women. In my *Heart-of-Hearts*, I knew that there was no real reason to feel that something was wrong between us. I decided that this time I wouldn't sabotage a relationship by copping a defensive attitude. I had to be wise, open, and disciplined enough to walk away from my old defensive behavior patterns and strategies, and explore the possibility—the probability—that this would not be a replay of the Melanie scenario.

I finally spoke to Deborah at about 4:00 P.M. I said, "Hi. What's going on?" She quickly began with, "Oh, Kenny, you can't imagine what happened last night! A few days ago, I'm sure someone followed me home in his car. When I got home last night after the party, my house was broken into. All of my drawers and closets were gone through. I was terrified. I didn't know if he was still waiting in the house. I ran out and called the police. I wound up at Jennifer's last night at about 2:00 A.M. I've been at the police station all day. I feel so violated and scared. Now I've got to move. It's a mess."

A lesson learned. I was presented with similar stimuli—someone I'm seriously dating not coming home all night after attending a party. But at *Crunch Time*, thank God, I stepped back and didn't assume that similar stimuli dictated the same outcome and the same response from me. They obviously didn't.

As I said, Deborah deserved my trust. I'm glad that I gave it to her and that I didn't just react by pursuing my usual course of behavior.

Strata-Gem:

Breaking up with old strategies and patterns of behavior can be very hard to do. But if you are to become the very best decision-maker possible, you must deal with facts rather than assumptions. You must be open to exploring various courses of action and be aware that even if you're presented with the same or similar stimuli as in the past, old ways of behaving may no longer be appropriate. After open, non-defensive exploration—and with discipline, courage, and vision—choose, and then stay with, the healthiest, wisest, and most effective *Strategies* and courses of action.

THE THREE "Ds" OF DECISION-MAKING: DESIRE, DISCIPLINE, AND DELAYED GRATIFICATION

DESIRE

If you aspire to achieve a goal, I have learned, seen, and counseled that *"You gotta really want it*," and you've got to be fully focused on attaining it. There's no question about it. Because if you lack either the strong desire or the focus, it will be too easy for you to be diverted into settling for more immediate and ultimately less gratifying substitutes.

Desire is an emotional word. It conjures up such energized qualities as "passion," "need," "want," and "belief." And when these emotional and sexual energies are channeled toward healthy and constructive ends, they can have a huge positive impact upon your goal-attaining efforts. These energies can initially have a catalyzing effect upon you. Thereafter, they can help you to sustain your efforts and focus as you face problems, crises, distractions, and weak moments . . . as we all inevitably do.

You cannot be tentative or defensive about what you want in order to hide your true feelings from yourself or from others in case you fail or fall short. On the contrary, you must clearly identify your goals, and not be afraid to put yourself on the line in your efforts to achieve them.

In your quest to identify and attain your goals, you must not only identify your most important values, but you must also identify, feel, and tap into your deepest desire and passion for goal attainment. You will need all of the desire and focus that you can muster when trying to incorporate the other two "Ds" of decision-making—*discipline* and *delayed gratification*—into your behavioral repertoires.

People who are successful know what they want, have the drive and focus to go after it, and have the tenacity to stay the course and follow through with their chosen plan of action.

Strata-Gem:

In order to achieve your goals, you must have the *desire*, the *focus*, and the *tenacity* to achieve them.

DISCIPLINE

In his best-selling book *The Road Less Traveled*, Dr. M. Scott Peck writes, "Discipline is the basic set of tools we require to solve life's problems. Without discipline we can solve nothing!"

I agree. In almost all instances, individuals who achieve their goals know that the practice of discipline in their thinking and in their actions is an indispensable element of their *Strategies* for success.

Much of the career counseling that I have done in order to help my clients achieve their potential involves, in one way or another, the qualities of discipline and its soul mate, delayed gratification.

For example, just the other day, one of my clients, "Julianna," was summoned by her news director (the manager of her news department) to meet with him in his office. During the meeting, he asked whether Julianna would forgo her long-awaited two-week vacation so that she could fill in for the main weeknight anchor of her station.

When Julianna arrived back at her desk, she called me and explained the situation. As we always try to do, Julianna and I examined the appropriate values and behavior options in an orderly, objective, and careful manner. We each wrote them down.

Her values were that she and her husband had planned and paid for their upcoming vacation months in advance, and neither one of them had taken a vacation for about a year. They both needed and wanted one. On the other hand, Julianna and I knew that the main anchor at her station would retire in the next few months, and that Julianna was the front-runner to replace her.

However, we both were aware that there was another female anchor at the station, "Cindy," who was also a candidate for the position, and that Cindy had openly made her desire to attain the position known to management. Julianna also knew that if she took her vacation, Cindy would be assigned to fill in for the two weeks.

We continued to list Julianna's values: If she got the main anchor position, her annual income would certainly double, and maybe triple. She would also ascend to a very prestigious position in a city that she wanted to make her home for the long term. All of these values were of significant importance to her.

I then recounted a story. Years ago, another client of mine, "Rita," left for a week's vacation. On the Friday before she left, the news director of her station told us that upon Rita's return, she would be promoted from being a morning anchor to a weekday evening anchor, a position that she had worked very hard to secure for the past twelve years. During Rita's vacation, the noon anchor, "Beverly," who had been at the station for a little over a year, filled in on the broadcast that Rita was to be promoted to.

That week, the station manager allegedly stopped at a gas station on his way home, where the attendant told him that, "All of the guys here really like the redheaded woman (Beverly) you have anchoring this week." The next thing we knew, station management changed its collective mind and Rita *didn't* get the promotion upon her return from vacation. Beverly did. This turn of events was emotionally and professionally devastating to Rita.

Julianna got the point. The wrong decision regarding her vacation could cost her a great deal, professionally, financially, and emotionally. She then asked me: "We all know that I'm the front-runner for the job, right?" I answered, "Right." She continued, "So I shouldn't have to worry about taking a vacation and having Cindy fill in. The question is, do you think that she has any chance of blowing them away while I'm on vacation?" I answered that I felt that Cindy was indeed pretty good, and that you never know what can happen when you allow a variable that you don't have control over to enter into an equation. Therefore, there was a chance, however small, that letting Cindy fill in could indeed result in an undesirable outcome for us.

I then ended by saying that, "According to my calculation, the professional equation clearly weighs out in favor of opting to be disciplined and putting off your vacation for a while—even if it's needed and will cost some money to postpone. I wouldn't give Cindy the opportunity to show her stuff. However, only you can calculate the personal equation of the value to you and your husband of not taking your vacation together at this particular time. Your decision depends upon how much the personal values mean to you in this instance. Do they outweigh the professional?"

Ten minutes later, Julianna called me back after speaking with her husband. She'd decided that she would fill in for the two weeks and that she and her husband would take their vacation a couple of months later. She recognized that this was *Crunch Time* for her, and that she had to be disciplined—she had to delay the gratification of taking her vacation as originally scheduled.

Julianna had indeed made the right choice (according to her value system). Two months later, she was promoted to the main weeknight anchor position, and before she left on vacation, we negotiated a wonderful new deal for her, which, by the way, included reimbursement for the expenses that she and her husband incurred in postponing their vacation—plus an extra week of vacation each year.

Julianna has been extraordinarily successful at achieving many of her dreams. This is because she has developed healthy and constructive decision-making thought processes. She understands when discipline is required, and when and where it is appropriate, she practices it.

Most of my clients start out in small markets and move a number of times during their careers. Many work six and seven days a week. Some of my network correspondent clients travel more than 200 days per year. As I mentioned earlier, the clients who ascend to the highest rung may often be equally (and in some cases, less) naturally talented than others, but they may also be more disciplined than most. They understand and accept that they have to give up things of value now (their hometowns, leisure time, and the stability of their relationships, etc.) in order to attain, at some future date, something that they perceive is of greater value (i.e., their dreams).

When I began to lose weight as a youngster, I realized that if I maintained a diet of three big meals a day, which included starches, desserts, and other goodies, I'd continue to be fat. That's my metabolism. For as long as I can remember, I've always loved desserts, bagels and cream cheese, malts, ice cream, etc., but in time, I grew to value being fit and healthy even more. The element of discipline in my thinking and actions allowed me to grow thin and stay that way.

As a teenager, when I was playing in tennis tournaments throughout the country, there would usually be an exciting event or a party to attend each night. I often had to weigh whether I would go out and enjoy the festivities, or go to bed early and be physically and mentally at peak condition for the next day's match. (In reaching my decision, I always had to take into account the fact that I needed more rest than others to perform at my best.) With disciplined thinking, I almost always opted to get my rest. My value system in this instance was: "I've traveled throughout the country and have sacrificed and practiced for years to get here. I now have the opportunity to win. I have put myself in the best position possible to succeed, so don't be stupid and blow it at the end by going out to the party."

I have attained many of my goals and dreams by practicing appropriate discipline.

When I entered Harvard, I knew that I would be competing for grades with some very smart individuals. I knew that if I wanted to do well academically and also compete successfully on the tennis team, I would have to be disciplined about how I allotted my time. With discipline, I graduated magna cum laude and became captain and the number-one player on the varsity tennis team. I also won national titles in two sports during my college career.

Later in life when I left the prestigious William Morris Agency and established my own company, I knew that I'd have to be twice as good and effective on my own, because I no longer had the William Morris name and reputation behind me. For the first three years of my company's existence, I worked a minimum of six days a week. I put many pleasures on hold. My discipline has yielded great rewards (according to my value system).

I fully understand that not everyone desires to be as focused as I am, and not everyone has my value system. However, one thing is certain. Appropriate use of discipline in your thinking and in your behavior can be one of your greatest allies and decision-making *Strategies*, when trying to attain your most coveted goals and enhance your life.

Strata-Gem:

The appropriate use of *discipline* is an indispensable element in the attainment of personal and professional success and valid high self-esteem.

DELAYED GRATIFICATION

In tennis, especially on a slow clay court, where powerful serves and ground strokes (forehands and backhands) are much less likely to dominate, I've learned that you often have to be patient and set up your opening, by hitting a series of shots until you can find an opportunity to win the point. This I refer to as "keeping the ball in play" until the appropriate moment or opening is presented, and then seizing the opportunity to win the point.

In implementing the *Strategy* of keeping the ball in play, I incorporate the concept of *delayed gratification*.

Similarly, when I'm playing against someone who has a dominating serve, I have to not only figure out how to win my opponent's service game ("break" his or her serve), but I must also be disciplined enough to continue to win ("hold") the games that I serve, so that I can stay even with my opponent until I can win the set by winning a game that he or she serves. The concept of "holding" your serve until you can break your opponent's serve also involves delayed gratification. You have to mentally, physically, emotionally, and strategically keep hanging in until your opportunity to "break serve" is presented to you, and then you must strive to make the most of it (carpe diem!).

The concept of delayed gratification, like discipline, is an integral part of healthy, constructive, and enhancing decision-making.

In my experience as a career counselor, I too often see people who want to attain positive ends and grab the brass (*not* gold!!!) ring immediately. Today, we live in an MTV world of quick, visual bits of stimulation and an era of fast food. We also live in an often dysfunctional society, where many children and adults have been raised with little or no consistency and/or a negligible amount of love. They therefore want things and relationships *now*, because experience has taught them that, by tomorrow, these coveted things and "special" individuals may well be gone. As a result, many people hunger for and rely upon immediate gratification . . . even if the gratification, in the short- or long-term, proves to be worthless or unhealthy. *It is this indiscriminate hunger and fear of loss that can lead to poor and destructive decision-making.*

I can't begin to estimate the large number of bad professional and personal choices that I've seen people make because they wanted an inappropriate quick fix or immediate closure to a situation.

Sometimes, attaining immediate gratification is possible at no great subsequent cost. But in many instances, you have to patiently and proactively continue to lay a solid foundation before you can achieve your most precious goals. In these latter situations, you have to keep hanging on, winning some battles and losing some skirmishes, or vice versa—and continue learning from both experiences, before you can win the "war." Or, put another (athletic) way, *with discipline*, you must keep the ball in play until you get the right opening or opportunity, then go for it.

I have been involved in numerous situations that have proven that there are times in life when it's best to hang in and stay sharp long enough to learn what you truly do and don't want. During this growth process, values, perceptions, and information may change, and with these changes, your goals may be modified and reprioritized. For example, I represent a number of individuals who originally thought that their ultimate goal was to become a network correspondent. However, after they got a taste of anchoring a newscast or hosting a program, or saw others do it—and they discovered the perks that go along with those particular positions—their aspirations changed. Also, as people's life situations change, reporting for a network can lose its allure when you're asked to be on the road two hundred days or more each year. It can be great for a single person, but it may very well be much less attractive if you get married and/or have a family.

The key here is, you often have a much better opportunity to identify what you truly do want and then secure it if you have carefully and correctly laid the right foundation—and this often takes time, discipline, the appropriate step-by-step choreography, and the practice of delayed gratification.

There are also instances when you just have to keep going, even when there's no immediate payoff in sight. I counsel my clients that this *Strategy* requires the greatest discipline. It's sort of like driving a car in a blinding fog or through a blinding torrential downpour. You just have to keep a straight and steady course until there's a clearing. You have to be guided by the heartfelt belief that *"If you do things right and do the right things, the right things will happen."* Often, this turns out to be the case. (An illustration of this is the Matt Lauer/*Access Hollywood* story found later in this book.)

For me, there is no more vivid example of the fruits of incorporating the *Strategy* of delayed gratification into one's decision-making process than what has transpired during the last thirty years of my father's professional life. My dad has always been in amazing physical shape. Despite his excellent health and sharp mind, however, his department store company chose to retire him at sixty-seven years young. My dad, who's always been optimistic and competitive, had the wind knocked out of his emotional sails. He knew that he had so much more to give, but he wondered, "Where will a sixty-seven-year-old man find a new career?"

Although he never outwardly showed it, he was inwardly sad at the prospect that he might never work again, because he truly loved what he did, which was training buyers to purchase clothes "off-price." However, much to his credit, during his retirement, he stayed in top physical shape, read his professional journals, and kept up his relationships with the clothing manufacturers he had done business with for years. Even with no possible job prospects in sight, my dad swam, played tennis, and walked every day. He kept himself in tip-top condition by not having desserts or many fatty foods, and he got lots of rest. He often would tell me, when he'd pass up a dessert, "No one's gonna hire someone who looks old and acts old. It's a young person's world out there. I've got to stay young—at least in spirit—and keep myself in fighting shape."

Incredibly, three long years after my dad retired, one of his former buyers, Ben Cammarata, called him. Ben had since taken over as president of the Marshall's chain of stores, and he was about to start a company called T.J. Maxx. He wanted to know whether my dad would consider training his T.J. Maxx buyers—even for just a month or two—the way my dad had trained Ben and many other now-illustrious department store executives years earlier.

My dad was absolutely elated. He immediately accepted, and started his second career at age seventy. Being in great physical and mental shape and keeping his finger on the pulse of the merchandising business paid off royally for my dad and for Ben (who eventually became chairman of T.J.X. Companies, which now owns Marshalls and T.J. Maxx, among several other companies). Now, twenty-seven years later, my dad still works for T.J. Maxx, still makes valuable contributions, and still receives praise, raises, and bonuses at age *ninety-seven*.

This is a magnificent example of how my dad benefited—beyond anyone's wildest dreams—by constructively deciding to keep the ball in play and hold serve until he could break. He delayed gratification and stayed lean and in shape during his three years of forced retirement, and as a direct result, he is now tasting the very sweet fruits of great decision-making more than a quarter-century later.

He truly is my role model.

Another problem with opting for immediate gratification is that you often don't take advantage of the opportunity to experience and enjoy the process and journey of goal achievement. For example, I've seen too many broadcasters who are so focused on their next move, and then the next, that they take no time to enjoy the uniqueness and beauty of their current stage of development. They don't even take time to enjoy the city that they're in. It's a pity, because in all likelihood, they'll never be there again.

As in all other decision-making situations, the issues of whether it's appropriate to delay gratification, and for how long, is a matter of wisely and honestly balancing values. There are times to go for the gold and seize the moment, but there are other times when keeping the ball in play—until you can produce the right opening or that opening is produced for you—and *then* going for it will produce a healthier, more satisfying, and longer lasting result.

Strata-Gem:

- There are times when it is constructive and self-enhancing to decide not to seize the moment, but instead wait until a more appropriate and/or valuable result can be achieved—and then go for it.

- Often, the hardest time to delay gratification occurs when you must remain disciplined even when there is no clear end—or gold ring—in sight. Although this scenario may be the most challenging, it may nevertheless bring you the greatest and sweetest rewards.

THE CONTINUAL GATHERING, ANALYSIS, AND INTEGRATION OF NEW DATA

Becoming an Active "Student of Life"

Over the years, people have asked me about my evolution from a troubled child to a highly achieving, constructive individual. One factor was that as I started to achieve mastery over small things, and then over larger activities and goals—such as making breakfast for my father while my mother was in the hospital, learning to play paddle tennis and then consistently improving my game, and losing weight—those "victories" and the positive feelings that flowed from them fueled the fire within me to improve myself in every area that I could. They also significantly raised my feelings of self-esteem and self-worth.

The other question that I'm often asked is: *How did I do it?* One of the answers lies in this chapter.

There is no more important tool for positive change, growth, and constructive decision-making than the *Strategy* of continuing throughout your life to gather and analyze new data—ideas, experiences, insights, knowledge, etc.—and then to test that data against what you already know, believe, and use. Some of the questions that you can ask include: How does the new data compare to the data on which you previously based your decision? Is it better, more advantageous, and/or healthier for you? Will it be more helpful in attaining your goals? Does it enhance you? If the answers are yes, you must then decide how to most effectively integrate these insights, first into your thought and decision-making processes, and then into your behavioral repertoires.

As people who know me well will attest, the foundation for almost all of my real-life navigation skills and decision-making *Strategies* has come from my athletic experiences, specifically in tennis and paddle tennis. Unlike sports such as baseball, basketball, and football, where you have coaches on the sidelines to coach and counsel you, a singles player in paddle tennis and tennis is out there alone. You have only yourself to rely on. If you're tired, sick, or just having a bad day, either you suck it up and get it right, or you lose. There's no one on the bench to come in and take your place. It's a true situation of the survival of the fitter, smarter, more technically proficient, emotionally together, and more adaptable competitor. As a result of participating in these individual sports, I've learned to become self-reliant and self-deterministic—because if I don't do it right, no one else will do it for me.

When I'm on the tennis court, I have to continually assimilate data as I reach my decisions. For example: Where is the sun, and how will it affect me and my opponent when we serve? What court surface are we playing on (clay, grass, cement), and how fast is it? Which direction is the wind blowing? What are my opponents' strengths and weaknesses, the knowledge of which I've gleaned either from past experience and/or our pre-match warm-up? Depending on how the match progresses, which of my strategies should I continue to rely on, abandon, and/or modify?

An illustration of the assimilation and analysis of data occurred during one of my most memorable high school matches. It was a cool, gray, early April day in Brooklyn. Our varsity high school tennis team was about to play its first match of the season. As a junior, I was our team's number-one player, and I'd been in that position for the previous two years. During that time, I was able to overpower many of my opponents (my usual strategy), because I was often bigger and stronger than they were. Over the winter, I had practiced my forehand and backhand and had added more power to my serve. I was excited to unleash my new, stronger weapons by hitting the hell out of the ball to set up my openings.

When I arrived at the courts, I met my opponent. He was a 6'4" senior (three inches taller than I was). As we warmed up, I noticed that his forehand and backhand were flat and smooth. His execution of these strokes was picture perfect.

As we played, I pummeled the ball to his backhand and approached the net. He responded by effortlessly hitting a shot right past me. I tried approaching the net on his forehand. Like a machine, he countered with a bullet for another great shot. I then tried staying back on the "baseline" and trading ground strokes with him. Power vs. Power. That didn't work, either. He won the first set, 6–2.

At that point, I thought to myself: "Let's think this through. I'm pretty good, and if this guy's beating the hell out of me, either he must be *really* good, or I'm not picking up on some of his weaknesses. Therefore, the strategy that I'm using must be flawed. Since he's not nationally ranked and I haven't heard of him before, I need to hang in long enough to figure him—and a way to win—out. I have to keep changing my game, and my strategies until I get it right."

As the second set began, a wind started to whip up. I was used to playing in windy conditions, because I had played both tennis and paddle tennis near the ocean for years. I knew that hitting the ball with the wind at my back required that I hit my strokes with more topspin, and ease up on the power. When playing against the wind, I would increase the depth and strength of my shots.

An interesting thing occurred. I changed my game (my strategies), but he didn't, or couldn't, change his. When he was hitting with the wind at his back, his flat shots now sailed out. When he hit against the wind, his shots landed short, on my side of the court, allowing me to assume the offense much more easily and hit more forcing and winning shots. I also noticed that when the wind was at my back, and I reduced the pace and strength of my shots by looping them high over the net, he handled the shot poorly. I then realized that my opponent was strictly a very good *counterpuncher*, in that he fed off my pace beautifully. But when he had to generate his own pace, he couldn't do it nearly as well.

The wind continued to blow for about twenty minutes. Enough time for me to win the second set, 6–2. Then, suddenly, the wind died down. Time for a decision (*Crunch Time!*). I took a moment and reflected upon all that I had learned about my opponent during the match. I decided that even though the wind was no longer a factor, I would continue to float balls back to him and continue to upset his rhythm. I would try to win "ugly"—just "gut" the match out—rather than lose artfully, by trading hard forehands and backhands with him (and once again play to his strength). I won the third set, 6–1.

That match, perhaps more than any other, reinforced within me the *Strategies* of being open, flexible, adaptable, and poised, along with the *Strategy* of continually assimilating data, until I hit on the most constructive and enhancing *Strategies* that reflect my values and enable me to attain my goals. The lesson that I took from that match is that if another individual is better than I am at some, or many, things—if he or she has better techniques, strengths, and/or cerebral or emotional strategies—I will acknowledge them, appreciate them, and learn from them and from the experience. I will also try to integrate them into my repertoire of *Strategies*. If he or she isn't better than I am, it's my mission—through exploration, experimentation, assimilation, and poise—to find a way to *raise my game*—by improving my *Strategies*—and thus successfully meet the challenge.

As in athletics, when I'm on my game in business and in life, I continually seek to acquire new information about the individuals and events around me. I then try to assess the value of this information and, if appropriate, develop new and modified *Strategies* for behavior. What this involves is a *hunger* for new data and the clear acknowledgment that I don't know all there is to know. It also requires a willingness to modify or totally discard my unproductive, non-enhancing strategies and to try something new and hopefully, more effective. It means becoming a proactive *Student of Life*. I must be willing to say, "I don't always know what's right, but I'm open and anxious to be better." It involves a commitment to learn, along with the realization that some mistakes will be made when trying new things, but that ultimately, every mistake will at the very least be a learning experience that one day may well make me a more effective decision-maker and decision-executor.

In the Jewish religion, there are the two "high holidays" of Rosh Hashanah and Yom Kippur. Rosh Hashanah begins a ten-day period of reflection and study. It is intended to be an honest examination of the things that individuals have done right and well during the past year, and those that were done incorrectly or wrong, or could have been done better or perhaps omitted altogether. At the heart of this study is the premise that we are human and will never be perfect. We have and will continue to make mistakes. The key is to try to grow to be a little better and more thoughtful each year. The ten-day study period of these holidays ends on Yom Kippur, known as the Jewish New Year. At sunset, a horn called a *shofar* is blown, signifying that a new year has begun and a brand new canvas has been given to each of us to paint on. The hope is that we will grow to be wiser and more humane artists with each passing year.

My philosophy is that every day presents us with a "Rosh Hashanah" and a "Yom Kippur," in that we must constantly be open to objectively and non-defensively gathering new data, new perspectives, and gleaning greater understanding. We must continually reexamine and retest our old and current strategies for behavior, as well as our beliefs and perspectives of ourselves and others, to see if they are still appropriate and the best and most enhancing ones for us. We must consciously and continuously strive to grow to be better, smarter, and more understanding of everything and everyone who is relevant to us. Ideally, like "make your own" salad or dessert buffets, the results and use of your gathering, analyses, and integration of data, will be uniquely yours and reflect your highest personal ideals, goals, and values. Optimally, you will create and recreate *Strategies* that will be effective and constructive for you, that will lift you and will enhance you. But keep in mind that this process need not be a selfish one. The *Strategies* that you create and implement may well be ones that nurture and help others. Furthermore, as we touched on earlier and will discuss in detail later, if you can practice appropriate *self-love* in the values that you choose, in the decisions that you make, and in the actions that you take, you will be much more likely to extend yourself to and do good things for others.

There is a popular saying that "hindsight is 20/20." If you continue to gather and assimilate new and relevant data, and you decide which new data will improve your decision-making, there's a good chance that your "foresight" will be close to being "20/20," as well. This is because you will be equipped to make better and more educated and wiser decisions as to how to handle new situations, based upon your study and integration of past experiences and new data. This *Strategy* can ultimately lead to success in every area of your personal and professional life.

The key is that you must always be thinking, learning, adjusting, polishing, and re-creating. That is, truly being an active *Student of Life*. In the film *Jerry Maguire*, Tom Cruise said: "Breakdown . . . breakthrough" (he believed that his near mental *breakdown* resulted in his "breakthrough" memo or mission statement). As we will discuss later, really bad (or really good) experiences shouldn't be the only triggers or catalysts for us to have a breakthrough in our emotional or intellectual development. On the contrary, the smallest and most inconsequential experiences can produce profound lessons. The best decision-makers and strategists learn from everything and everyone. *They incorporate the best and incinerate the rest*.

Strata-Gem:

- There is no more important *Strategy* for your growth and your positive decision-making than continuing throughout your life to gather and analyze new experiences, ideas, insights, knowledge, etc., and then objectively test them against what you already know, believe, and do. By doing this, you can continually improve your decisions.
- Learn to be an active *Student of Life*. The knowledge and the wisdom that you'll gain will be invaluable and empowering.

"BIG PICTURE," CONTEXT-BASED THINKING

A few years ago, I played in the finals of the Men's National Open Paddle Tennis Doubles Championships, against the number one team in the country. The score was knotted at one set each. The final set was tied at eight games each, and we were in the midst of playing a tiebreaker. (Yes, *Crunch Time*.) During the "breaker," one of our opponents, who was the best overall paddle tennis player in the country, mixed up his shots and his strategy a bit more. (He had the confidence, the skill, and the flexibility to change his strategy at the appropriate time.) This caused us to not be as effective as we might have been otherwise. They won the tiebreaker, 7-5, and the title.

I had played as well as I could have hoped. I just needed to play some points more creatively. So, at thirty-eight years old, after a couple of national titles and a few second-place finishes under my belt, I decided that I needed to improve my game. I would study the national champions and see what I could learn about them and myself.

During the next tournament they played, I sat up in the stands and watched. It was fascinating. I saw things in the stands that I had never seen down on the court when I was playing against them. As Robin Williams said in *Dead Poets Society* after asking all of his students in his classroom to stand on their desks, "The view is much different from up here." From above, I saw how one of my opponents planted himself so close to the net that by lobbing over his head, we could get his partner out of position enough so that, as a team, they might become more vulnerable. I gleaned a number of other new perspectives, possibilities, and alternatives from my seat in the stands.

At the end of a day of viewing, a thought about some broadcasters whom I knew came to mind. I realized that some of the most talented communicators, with the biggest and brightest futures, were getting much too caught up with minor day-to-day hassles. These problems were bringing them down emotionally. I realized that somehow they weren't seeing the *Big Picture*—that these incidents, when taken in the context of their extraordinary broadcasting careers, would mean absolutely nothing. In the *Big Picture*, these skirmishes wouldn't have the impact of the smallest zit on an elephant's back. (I discuss this, in the sad story below.) I often thought to myself, "God, these people have everything going for them. They just need to see the *Big Picture* of their careers the way I do. They would enjoy the process so much more." They could also be more selective in the battles that they *did* choose to fight. I realized that because I wasn't fighting "on the ground"—day to day—as they were, but was instead viewing their careers more objectively from the stands, I had a different, fuller, broader and, in many respects, better perspective than they had. A perspective that was incredibly enlightening when it came to effective problem-solving and decision-making.

The lesson was: *Far too often, while fighting our day-to-day battles on the ground, we never look beyond ourselves, or the immediate moment, situation, need or craving at hand.* Therefore, we fail to view things from the fuller, richer, wider context of the *Big Picture*. I have seen and been involved in so many instances where better perspectives and new spins and solutions could either be discerned or created if the individuals involved would have taken some time to look at and examine the *Big Picture*—that is, to step away from the heat and angst of the moment and calmly, objectively, and creatively study the landscape, the players, and their past strategies and agendas in the context of the situation that they're involved in and/or the decision that they are in the process of making.

For example, one of the saddest and most disappointing stories that I've seen unfold in broadcast journalism involved a woman whom

I believe had as much talent and as many good things going for her as any individual I've ever encountered in television news. Everyone but she recognized this, even though it was clearly evident that her career was on a meteoric rise. Because of her deep-seated insecurities, she would continually obsess about all of the jealous individuals in the newsroom, when, in the *Big Picture*, all she needed to focus on was her continued growth. In the *Big Picture*, none of these other "competitors" and jealous individuals would be factors in determining whether or not she would fulfill her extraordinary potential. However, she could never see the *Big Picture* of her career the way that I and almost everyone else did. As a result, she allowed other less than well-meaning individuals to drive her crazy. In the end, this incredibly talented woman self-destructed, and she and her potentially extraordinary career plummeted into oblivion.

Big Picture thinking and decision-making will play a major role throughout the remainder of our journey.

The *Big Picture* As It Relates to Truly Responsive Decision-Making

So often, I see people who just don't get it or can't see it. In many instances, they make insensitive and destructive decisions, and act in incorrect and inappropriate ways, given the circumstances.

For example, I know many individuals who are so defensive, egocentric, and/or insensitive that almost all of their interpersonal decisions are based solely upon their own defensive perceptions, needs, and expectations. They never seem to take other people's perspectives, strategies, or values into account, or consider the differences in nuances from one situation to another. Therefore, they are never able to seek out or attain a "win-win" result. Nor does it occur to them to examine the whys and the wherefores of their too-often dysfunctional strategies for dealing with people.

Essentially, these individuals are so self-centered, scared, and/or defensive that they don't see beyond themselves or the unique problem that's immediately facing them. They have psychologically myopic vision and make their decisions in a vacuum, often blindly relying on their old, inappropriate, and diminishing strategies.

As a result, although these individuals are technically very good at what they do, they often lose and/or upset many clients, business associates, and others whom they deal with, because their behavior is non-responsive and insensitive to their clients' and business associates' needs and expectations. They are clueless as to the correct perception of others, as well as to how others truly perceive them.

If those individuals could see and understand their own behavior a little more clearly, and if they could take the time to see the *Big Picture* of how their flawed strategies and decisions have consistently left people wanting, angry, and critical of them, they might put two and two together and conclude that some strategy reworking is in order. However, as far as I can tell, in most instances, they remain unaware and insensitive. Their defensive and destructive perspectives and strategies keep them out of touch. As a result, they just don't see it and rarely get it. And unfortunately—and to the regret of many—unless these individuals gain enough awareness to constructively rework their strategies, they will never come close to fulfilling their enormous potentials.

For example, later on we'll discuss an executive named John, who was so focused on not allowing any of his assistants to grow, for fear that he'd appear less important or valuable to his employers, that he failed to see how, in the *Big Picture*, he was stifling his company's growth and development, and ultimately sabotaging his own.

As we discussed earlier, seeing the *Big Picture* is metaphorically analogous to cerebrally, emotionally, and psychologically leaving your body and, for a few moments, floating in air in such a way as to have an expansive overall view of things. You thereby endeavor to visualize the performance of your past and present strategies, how you have fared using those strategies, and how the individuals who you are presently dealing with might be affected by those strategies. By discovering, assimilating, and assessing this data in an objective, constructive way, you're able to much more effectively decide whether the current situation that you are facing requires you to stick with your old strategies, to modify them, or to craft completely new ones.

On the other hand, if you don't take the time and/or make the effort to see the *Big Picture* when you're making your decisions, you may well reflexively stick with your same old strategies, which may or may not have been appropriate at one time, but are clearly inappropriate in the situation that you're currently dealing with. In my "Deborah" scenario that I described earlier, I chose to step away and truly examine the *Big Picture* of my past patterns of behavior in the context of the unique situation that I was facing. I then correctly decided that my old strategy (of playing the victim) was no longer appropriate in that (and probably in any other) context. By figuratively going up in the air and seeing the bigger, grander *Picture*, I was able to make an effective and responsive decision.

There are indeed times when considering just yourself is an appropriate and effective decision-making *Strategy*. However, there are many other instances in which considering some or all of the following thirteen questions is a *Strategy* that, more than any other, will enable you to fashion truly constructive and efficacious decisions.

I have time after time seen great decision-makers look beyond themselves and the immediate problem or challenge they're facing. They take the time to consider a number of relevant elements. When you are trying to craft the most responsive decision, honestly identify and explore the following questions, depending upon their appropriateness, in the context of the decision that you're faced with:

1) Who will be affected by the decision at hand?
2) What are your values and priorities, as well as those of the other individuals involved with or affected by the decision?
3) What are your short- and long-term goals, and what are those of the other individuals involved with or affected by the decision?
4) What have your experiences taught you? What experiences might others involved or affected by the decision have had in a similar situation? And, as a result, what might their expectations about your course of action be?

5) Are your old strategies still—or have they ever been—appropriate, healthy, and positively productive ways of acting in situations such as this one? What might the strategies of the other individuals involved in or affected by the situation be?

6) What are the various courses of action that you might take in the given instance? What courses of action might others consider taking and expect you to take?

7) If possible, and when appropriate, can this be turned into a win-win situation and/or result?

8) What are your fears and defenses regarding the situation and decision at hand? What might the fears and defenses of others be?

9) How will others be affected by the course of action that you choose?

10) What does your intellect tell you is the correct course of action to take?

11) What does your *Heart-of-Hearts* tell you is the right decision?

12) What new information is gleaned by taking a step or two back, going up in the air, and looking at the long-term, *Big Picture* of your life, and how will this particular decision fit into that *Picture*? Will it better enable you to achieve your most cherished long-term goals?

13) In light of all of this, what is the wise, constructive, and most enhancing course of action to take?

The *Strategy* of viewing decisions through the richer perspective of the *Big Picture*, has enabled me, my clients, and many others to maintain healthy courses of action during the most trying of times; act positively and with poise to what may appear at times to be some very painful private and public setbacks; and to deal with a myriad of positive and negative stimuli wisely, flexibly, and creatively, and in a constructive and orderly manner.

I am 100 percent sure that I have become a much more effective and successful counselor and person by making the effort to objectively understand where others are coming from, integrating this information into my decision-making equations and then fashioning tailor-made, appropriate decisions and actions in direct response to the particular situation that I'm dealing with. Engaging in *Big Picture, Context-Based Thinking* is one of the *Strategies* by which I and my successful clients arrive at success-evoking conclusions.

By considering the *Big Picture* when making your decisions, you are much less likely to make a quick-fix or hasty decision. This is so because one of the criteria for making a *Big Picture* decision is: *How will your decision effect you and/or the situation at hand in the long run?* This point is crucially important because you must always remember that your decisions may well not just impact you today; you may have to live with them over time, and sometimes, for the rest of your career, marriage, relationship, or life.

Additionally, by seeing your life in the rich context of the *Big Picture*, I believe that you will enjoy things so much more, because you won't be brought down by the small stuff—the inevitable daily problems, challenges, and setbacks that we all face. As I mentioned earlier, I see people brought down far too often by so many small irritants that in the *Big Picture* amount to nothing that they don't enjoy all of the gifts, potential, and opportunities that they do have. In essence, they fail to enjoy their biggest gift: their life, with all its trials and tribulations. On this point, the other night I saw Billy Crystal's docu-film, *61 about the race by Mickey Mantle and Roger Maris to break Babe Ruth's record of sixty home runs in a season. I found it to be a wonderfully insightful story detailing the personalities and psyches of both Mantle and Maris.

One segment of the film focused on the fact that Mantle (who had many wonderful natural gifts, as well as many self-destructive strategies) had a way with people, especially the working press. As a result, the press loved him. Maris, on the other hand, hid from the press and the limelight. This often led to criticism by the press, which he internalized. The movie portrayed how much Mantle relished and appreciated every moment of his quest to break Ruth's record. Maris, on the other hand, hated all the attention he received and the pressure he felt—so much so that his hair began to fall out.

I raise this story here because it illustrates so clearly what a great difference one's point of view can make. As Maris came ever-closer to breaking Ruth's long-standing and much-revered record, he appeared absolutely miserable. One newsman commented that he couldn't believe that Maris couldn't see that this was a once-in-a-lifetime experience to cherish (the *Big Picture*). Maris was getting paid a good salary to play for the crème de la crème, the New York Yankees, and go out and hit home runs—which he was doing much more prolifically than anyone who had played before him—while others had to do such things as pick up garbage to earn a living. What the writer couldn't understand was how Maris had become so caught up in the angst of being asked question after question, over and over again, that he failed to enjoy any part of his record-setting journey. How sad, because Maris never saw the *Big Picture* of how much excitement and controversy he was generating throughout the country.

Strata-Gem:

Viewing things in the insightful context of the *Big Picture* can help you put things in their proper perspective for both the short and long terms and make you a wiser and more constructive decision-maker.

IDENTIFYING AND WEIGHING YOUR MOST
IMPORTANT AND ENHANCING VALUES:
"WHAT WILL MAKE YOUR HEART SING?"

Obviously, one of the most important steps in making a constructive and an enhancing decision is: *You've got to know what you want.* What is it that you truly desire to accomplish, avoid, change, secure, etc. with your decision? Or, as I always ask my clients, when I want to know what their ultimate career dream is, "What will make your heart sing?"

Although this sounds easy, it often isn't. Making the most constructive and efficacious decision involves identifying a number of important and attractive values and goals. Then you must carefully and as objectively as possible weigh their relative positive and negative value to you, by honestly and non-defensively thinking things through and searching your *Heart-of-Hearts* for the true answers.

Matt's Mammoth Decision

When Matt Lauer and I met for the first time and he was considering whether he wanted to employ me as his broadcasting representative, I asked him what, in his *Heart-of-Hearts*, he aspired to do and be. Because Matt was between jobs at that point and hadn't yet met with any real, consistent on-air success, he half-kiddingly responded that he would be happy to just hold a job for more than thirteen weeks. (Many a truth is said in jest!) I then tried to dig deeper, and inquired, "C'mon, Matt, what will really make your heart sing?" He confided that he would one day love to host the *Today* show *or Good Morning America*, or be Larry King.

Up to that point in Matt's career, he had hosted and/or reported on "lighter" shows, such as *P.M. Magazine* and *HBO Entertainment News*. He had also hosted a New York City–based program called *9 Broadcast Plaza*. It was seeing Matt on this show that made me believe that he could indeed attain his dream of hosting one of the network morning news programs. However, Matt had never anchored or reported "hard news" on a regular basis before. So, at that stage of his career, he was viewed as an entertainment-type personality. This would have been fine if Matt had wanted to secure a position on a show such as *Entertainment Tonight*. The problem was that Matt's true dream was to host *Today* or *Good Morning America*, and this required that he have the ability to conduct insightful and compelling hard news and breaking-news interviews and reporter debriefings. However, neither Matt nor I had anything on his resume or on tape that would prove that he could successfully do this in a hard news format. So we decided over lunch that the optimal *career choreography* would be for him to somehow begin his news career in New York City, where he was living, which is the number-one market in the country. This generally would be an almost impossible goal to achieve, but the fact that New York City viewers were already familiar with him made it more of a possibility. We agreed that the perfect position for him would be to one day anchor a newscast such as WNBC-TV's popular *Live at Five*, which featured "live" daily interviews. As a result, he could grow as a news anchor and develop and hone his harder-edged interviewing skills on the same show.

With some time and some extraordinary good fortune, Matt secured a weekday morning news anchoring and interviewing position on WNBC in New York. He was a natural. Within weeks, he was temporarily assigned to anchor the weekend morning newscast as well. Soon thereafter, his role was expanded, incredibly, to anchoring *Live at Five*—just as we had discussed two years earlier.

The next step in the choreography was for me to secure for Matt an opportunity to fill in as a host of the *Today* show. The huge obstacle was that the executives of NBC's news division, which has jurisdiction over *Today*, perceived Matt as a talented, handsome news anchor and interviewer with no real major national or international hard news experience. As a result, they denied my first request for Matt to fill in. In this instance, I needed to do some creative decision-making. (For an in-depth discussion of this topic, please see the upcoming chapter on "Out-of-the-Box Decision-Making.") I decided to fly from Los Angeles to Miami to visit the executive vice president of news for NBC, Don Browne. Don and I had recently put together a number of successful deals, and I considered him a wise and valued friend. I half-kiddingly told Don that I wouldn't leave Miami, or his side, until he agreed to give Matt an opportunity to fill-in as host on *Today*. By the end of a very enjoyable couple of days, he agreed to give Matt his shot. A day or two later, Matt received a call from the brilliant *Today* show executive producer, Jeff Zucker, confirming this.

Matt's hosting debut was a home run. Soon after, he was filling in on the *Today* show regularly. He then was offered the news reader position (where he would also serve as the regular fill-in for Bryant Gumbel) on the *Today* show. The decision to be a member of the coveted *Today* show and leave local news was a no-brainer, because it was the absolutely right next career step. However, about a year or so later, Matt was faced with a huge decision.

By that time, Matt was gaining great popularity on the *Today* show—especially as a fill-in host. However, his success was conflicting in some ways—at least for me. It was Matt's dream to be the host of *Today*, but Matt is as loyal a friend as anyone can be. He has incredible character, and he would do absolutely nothing—nor allow me to do anything—that would undermine his very close friend Bryant. So I couldn't lobby for Matt to take Bryant's job, even though many individuals—including some NBC execs—felt and confided to me that the *Today* show might be even more successful with Matt as a host. Trust me, the kind of loyalty that Matt showed is extremely rare, in any business. (This situation is discussed in more depth in the *Step 5* chapter.)

Then came the bomb. One of the heads of NBC called Matt and

told him that the network was starting an entertainment show on the West Coast called *Access Hollywood*. It would be a first-rate, weeknight show competing with *Entertainment Tonight*. NBC wanted Matt to leave the *Today* show, move to Los Angeles, and host *Access* with another client of mine, Giselle Fernandez. This show, the exec promised, would be a top priority for NBC and receive tremendous promotion. Knowing what Giselle was earning as a host of *Access*, I knew that Matt would certainly double and possibly triple his *Today* show salary. One NBC executive went so far as to tell Matt that if Bryant's job ever came available, he could come back to New York and host *Today*.

Talk about having conflicting values and needing to very carefully and honestly explore and weigh those values. This decision was a killer, but not, as it turned out, for the obvious reasons. First of all, being the main cohost of a show such as *Entertainment Tonight* or *Access Hollywood* was a position that Matt, years earlier, had coveted and aspired to. And because his background had been in entertainment news, he had always felt, prior to joining WNBC and NBC news, that it would be much more realistic to fulfill his dream in the entertainment news arena than it would in hard news.

Another consideration for Matt was that the host position on *Access Hollywood* was a bird in the hand. The job was his, whereas the *Today* show was number one in the morning show ratings, and there was every reason to expect that Bryant would continue as its host for the next ten or twenty years. So Matt could well have weighed his values and stated the issue before him as follows: "Do I take the main hosting job of *Access Hollywood* (a position he would have been thrilled to secure up until he began his news career a couple of years earlier), or do I stay on the *Today* show as its news reader and fill-in host for years to come?

Also added to Matt's decision-making equation were the values of the substantial increase in salary that he would receive to host *Access*, and the great desire of NBC executives, who had been good to Matt, to have Matt host *Access* and get it off to a successful start. This latter value, as it turned out, was the most important one to Matt, because he didn't want NBC to perceive his decision not to accept the

Access Hollywood offer as either a sign that he was ungrateful for all that NBC had done for him or as a slap in the network's face. He felt this way for two reasons: One, because he truly appreciated NBC's support, and two, because he didn't want to lose that support when future, and possibly more appropriate, growth opportunities presented themselves.

When Matt called me about the *Access* offer, he had already discussed it with others. After recounting his conversations with various NBC executives, Matt asked me for my perspective. He suggested that I call him back after I had time to think things through. Later that day, I called Matt with my thoughts, I said, "Matt, do you remember the day that we first got together? You told me that hosting the *Today* show or *Good Morning America* was your dream. You never mentioned *Entertainment Tonight*. You said that hosting a morning news program was your choice, even though, at that point in your career, hosting a program such as *Entertainment Tonight* was much more realistic than the *Today* show. But all that's changed, because you're now an integral part of the kind of show that you would one day love to host. I also know how attractive hosting *Access Hollywood* can be, and how much fun you might have doing it. The question is, what in your *Heart-of-Hearts* will make your heart sing *today*? (No pun intended!) Search deep and decide what you truly value. Both choices are great, but one may be more right and appropriate for where you are at this stage of your life and career development."

Matt, who is one of the most emotionally intelligent individuals I know, answered my question without any hesitation; he wanted to stay and host the *Today* show, even though Bryant didn't appear to be going anywhere, and he would do nothing to usurp him. Matt just needed to find a way not to make NBC management upset with him because of his decision to decline their impassioned plea to host *Access*.

I then added the following three thoughts to help make Matt's decision to forgo *Access Hollywood* easier for him to live with.

First, I said, even if Bryant stays at the *Today* show for years to come, it doesn't mean that Charlie Gibson won't retire or leave *Good Morning America*, and who is a better candidate than Matt Lauer to replace him? Matt came back with the reasonable counterargument that he still had years left on his NBC contract, so who knows if the timing of *GMA*'s need to fill Charlie's position and Matt's contract expiration would coincide?

Good point.

My second thought was that I disagreed with the NBC executives who had implied that if Bryant left *Today*, Matt could come back from *Access Hollywood* to host *Today*. My perception of the then-president of NBC news was that he already had concerns about Matt's news credibility—especially during times of crisis. If Matt went to *Access*, he would dig his own grave, by losing *all* news credibility in the eyes of the NBC news president. I believed that if Bryant left the *Today* show, and Matt was hosting *Access Hollywood*, a "newsman" such as Brian Williams would succeed Bryant.

My third point was that if Matt followed his heart, by discerning what his true values were, and if he was good at what he did (which he would be), the money would come. So the disparity between what *Access* would pay Matt and what he was earning as the newsreader on *Today* was a consideration, but not a major one.

Matt then interjected, "Ken, the money isn't an issue. I grew up watching the *Today* show, and to host it one day is my dream. And I'm on the right track. You and I both agree. I'm staying. Let's hope it's the right decision and that NBC's not upset."

A year later, Bryant Gumbel left the *Today* show, and Matt replaced him. The ratings increased substantially, and Matt is as happy in his position as one can possibly be. By digging deep and effectively weighing his most heartfelt values, and by keeping his eyes on his most cherished prize, Matt is living his dream. This couldn't happen to a more deserving or better person.

My Weighty Decision

I was a fat kid. So fat that I can still picture one of my friends counting the rolls of fat around my stomach as I sat with my shirt off at the beach.

Then there was the day when I went into the neighborhood diner to buy some M&Ms and other chocolate candies, and the owner condescendingly said, in a voice loud enough for all those having lunch at the counter to hear, "Do you really need that?" At that moment, all of the customers turned to look at me. Some laughed. Others gave me disapproving looks. I was mortified. My face must have turned seven shades of red. I quickly escaped from the diner, candyless. Feelings of hurt and embarrassment filled my insides as tears streamed down the outside.

These and other once-painful food- and weight-related experiences will always be etched into my memory.

Thereafter, wherever I went, I was self-conscious about the way that I looked, and about what and how much I ate. Whenever I consumed something fattening or asked for seconds, I felt that all eyes descended upon me in a disapproving way. Frequently, I was the brunt of kids' jokes. I recall all too well how I had to shop in the "husky" department when buying clothes. In some instances, clothes that my friends wore weren't available in my size, and when they were, they never seemed to look as good on me.

I remember that for the longest time the store that we shopped at didn't carry white jeans in my size. And I desperately wanted to wear white jeans just like my thin friends did. When my mom and I finally located some, my thighs and butt appeared so big in them that I looked like a cross between a giant white pear and a tent. I *hated* my thighs. So as excited as I was to find a pair that fit me, I was too embarrassed to wear them.

Between the ages of nine and eleven, I would often stop off after school for custard éclairs or a piece of cheesecake. Ice cream each afternoon was a given. Devouring second and third helpings of macaroni and cheese or spaghetti and meat sauce at school lunches made my day. And whenever something caused me angst or fear, I'd retreat into my room with a big bag of M&Ms or Oreos and assuage those uncomfortable feelings. In essence, when any of these goodies were around, like Pavlov's dog, I'd salivate and automatically react, by eating *all* that was available.

Then, at about twelve, I really became serious about paddle tennis. I loved playing the game and I was good at it. Things started to change. I lost some weight and finally began to develop mastery over an activity. This helped me to gradually develop valid feelings of self-esteem and a positive self-image. I received positive feedback and reinforcement as never before. Girls paid more attention to me—and for a change, it wasn't because of my misbehavior or my jokes at the expense of others.

Soon thereafter, I adopted a new mind-set and perspective. I began to explore and analyze my past behaviors and values, and I realized that some of them were no longer constructive and enhancing. I also tried to identify my true values and desires. I realized that I wanted to feel good about myself, be great at paddle tennis, be attractive to others, etc. Then one day I asked myself if the short-term values of the good taste of all of those foods and the momentary enjoyment of eating them were worth the weight that I'd gain. Was the pleasure of eating fattening foods more or less valuable to me than:

- Being more successful athletically? (Keeping in mind that when I was lighter, I was faster, more agile, and had more stamina.)

- Looking better and being more physically attractive?

- Feeling infinitely better about myself?

- Being able to wear the clothes that I wanted to wear, and looking better in them?

- Being able to eat without others scrutinizing what or how much I consumed?

The resounding answer, when I polled my *Heart-of-Hearts*, was that I liked being thinner much better.

From that day onward, when presented with M&Ms, éclairs, macaroni and cheese, and the like, I'd step away and remember what I really wanted and truly valued. I declined eating fattening food more and more as my values became clearer and stronger, and the results of my discipline became more tangible and elating. Success inspired more discipline, which in turn resulted in more success. In every way, I loved being thinner. Sometimes, I'd slip and take one or two steps backward with every two or three steps forward (breaking up with old habits and emotional crutches, after all, *is* hard to do). But eventually, the stronger, constructive values won out. For the past thirty-eight years, I've remained disciplined and thin. And when I *do* begin to gain weight, my values and the perception of how I want to look and feel, enable, empower, and compel me to immediately modify my eating habits, and intelligently increase my exercise regimen.

Over the years, while some of my values regarding my diet have remained the same, others have changed. I still want to compete athletically at the highest level possible; I still want to look good personally and professionally; and I still enjoy feeling good about myself. But I have also added two values to my list: good health and longevity.

Ever since I can remember, my dad has cherished his health and has done things such as walking instead of taking cabs or driving. With great discipline, he exercises regularly, whether it's walking an hour each day, swimming, or ice skating. Through the years, I've seen him walk in the rain and snow just to keep himself fit. My dad doesn't smoke and he is careful to get enough sleep. By valuing his health, my dad, at the age of ninety-seven, is able to work three days a week. He continues to be sharp and fit, has a great zest for life, and derives the most possible out of his life.

My dad is a role model for hundreds of twenty-five- to forty-year-old buyers because of his intimate and vast knowledge of his business, creative negotiating strategies, youthful appearance, high energy level, and contagious enthusiasm. My dad has missed only three or four days of work over the past twenty-seven years. And while genetics have no doubt played a significant role in his good health and longevity, his high value and regard for his physical well-being through the years have also been major factors in his celebration of healthy and vital living.

According to *my* value system, no dessert, no serving of macaroni and cheese (no matter how good), and no other fattening food or drink outweighs being fit and healthy. Conversely, I can't think of anything worse than spending my time in a hospital having bypass surgery (or any other related procedure), or being operated on for lung cancer or liver problems, because I had consciously chosen to continually eat rich foods or smoke or drink alcohol excessively.

Some individuals may counter my disciplined value system with the value of "Why not live for today and enjoy it all, as we may not be here tomorrow?" My perspective is: There's a good chance that I *will* be here tomorrow, and I want to give myself the best chance not only to be here for *many* tomorrows, but also to be healthy enough to truly make the most of them, as my dad has.

Instances when I choose to turn down fattening and rich foods, cigarettes, recreational drugs, and excessive alcohol are ideal opportunities for me to make constructive decisions according to my value system, and to take tangible ownership regarding the quality and length of my life.

As individuals who achieve their goals know, the key is to do those things that will put you (and those whom you desire to help) in the very best position possible to succeed.

Making healthy, enhancing, value-based decisions accomplishes this.

In the "Subjectivity" chapter, I will discuss a number of decisions for which I had to honestly identify and weigh my values in order to make the best choices from the information available to me. The strongest example of this may have been the time I had a wonderful opportunity to leave college in my sophomore year and join the pro tennis circuit, while being coached by Gardner Malloy, a world famous player and instructor. After considering and weighing my values and choices during a most agonizing scenario, I opted to stay in school and forgo giving the pro tennis circuit a focused shot. In that instance, I know that I weighed my values honestly and correctly. My decision definitely set the path for me to reach my current position of representing many of this country's most talented broadcast journalists, a career that I cherish.

The message in all of this? It is of the utmost importance to take the opportunity and make the necessary effort to dig deep and search your heart and soul, sincerely and honestly, in order to clearly identify the truest and highest values of your *Heart-of-Hearts*. Truth and clarity are essential components to success here. Recognizing and knowing what you truly want for yourself is a key to making wiser decisions before, after, and during *Crunch Time*—and this key will propel and compel you to stick with your decisions—even during crisis periods.

This formula has worked wonders for me and my clients over the years.

As we discussed in the previous chapter, it is one of your primary goals to continually assimilate data, to compare that data with the prior information and perceptions that you had and have, and to decide whether you need to maintain, modify, or discard your old behavior patterns. By engaging in this process, you put yourself in the best position possible to have your decisions and subsequent actions reflect and stay true to your most cherished values and goals. Implicit in all of this is that you truly know what your most important and heartfelt values and goals are.

If you are going to make decisions that reflect your "highest" self and your heartfelt values, you must continually mine the truth. You must know what you truly want. *It's of the utmost importance to regularly take some quiet time and to make a conscious effort to be in touch with your true feelings and passions, because they will be your very best decision-making guides.*

Strata-Gems:

- In order to make the most constructive and enhancing decisions, identify and weigh your most important values and goals.
- If you are to be the most proactive and effective decision-maker possible, you must stay in touch with your true values and dreams. You must know what these values are, and if they've changed, you must determine why they've changed. Just as a heart monitor keeps us constantly apprised of a person's heart condition, you must continually monitor and be aware of the status of your *Heart-of-Heart's* desires.

PRIMARY VERSUS SECONDARY
DECISION-MAKING REASONS

As a career counselor who above all wants to see his clients happy and fulfilled, I'm called upon many times a day to help clients reason-through their decisions. Unfortunately, I cannot begin to count the number of times that very smart people attempt to make decisions based upon the wrong reasons.

In advising my clients, I often separate reasons into two categories: *primary reasons*, which reflect one's true *Heart-of-Hearts* feelings, values, and goals; and *secondary reasons*, which don't.

An example of someone making a professional decision based upon a secondary reason involved a newscaster who took a job (against my counsel) as a field reporter in a particular city, because he had heard that the city was beautiful and that it had lots of single women. The problem was that the job description of the new position didn't include any regular or fill-in anchoring. Up to that point in his career, my friend had been a very successful news anchor, and he loved anchoring. From the day that he started the new job, he worked exclusively as a reporter, for about fourteen hours a day, six days a week. After three months or so, he called to tell me that he was miserable at work. He was feeling that he shouldn't have taken a job that he wasn't truly excited about, even though it might have been a way to possibly meet Ms. Right or to enjoy a skyline. Because of his heavy schedule, he barely had any time to do either. When he did have some time, he was either too unhappy or too tired to enjoy either. He concluded that he should have taken or declined the job based only upon the primary reason that this was, or was not, the right job for him.

Eventually, he extricated himself from his station contract, and he is now happily anchoring in another city. He has a steady girlfriend whom he's crazy about, and I've sent him posters of skylines of beautiful cities.

Another instance of an individual making a decision based on secondary reasons occurred in college where I had a close friend, Scott. Within weeks of becoming roommates, I came home from class on three separate occasions to find Scott either throwing up or hyperventilating. After the third instance, I invited him out to dinner to see if I could help. I learned that Scott, who had one of the highest grade-point averages in our class, had been accepted into medical school—but dreaded going. He had no interest in studying or practicing medicine. Apparently he chose pre-med as his major in response to the intense, lifelong pressure heaped on him by his mother to become a doctor. She would accept nothing less. This unhealthy situation was compounded by the great amount of positive attention that he received from the undergraduate coeds (aka "pre-weds"), who either knew or were told (by him) that he was pre-med and at the top of his class. Scott loved the attention that he received and the exalted position that he was accorded by being Harvard's strongest candidate for acceptance into Harvard's and/or Yale's medical schools. The big problem was that Scott pursued medicine for the secondary reasons of pleasing and placating his mother and attracting women (who were interested in Scott for their own secondary reasons—his degree, his status, and his future earning potential).

Because Scott made the decision to pursue medicine for secondary reasons, he hated his life and became physically ill. With time and further conversations, Scott decided to defer his admission to medical school, and he eventually declined the opportunity for good. Instead, he pursued his real passion—painting—a great primary reason. Today, Scott is a successful artist. He is happy and much healthier, physically and emotionally. He has also found a mate who appears to be with him for the primary reason that she loves him, not because she loves being with a would-be doctor or an artist.

While in his early thirties, another of my former college roommates quit his position as the comptroller of a major national company to become a high school teacher and to help his very accomplished wife raise their three terrific daughters. He teaches because he loves it, he is the world's most loving father, he and his wife are best friends— and he is one of my heroes. He entered into all of these relationships for primary reasons. He earns less money as a teacher, but he has been true to himself and to those around him, and as a result, he appears to be at peace and quite happy.

Everyone who aspires to achieve their life goals generally has to perform some tasks that he or she may not like. This comes with the territory. However, when and if you make significant life-goal decisions based upon secondary instead of primary reasons, you usually don't enjoy the goal attainment process much, if at all, and the ultimate payoff is often hollow. Whereas when you pursue activities for true primary reasons, you feel congruent and in harmony with your heartfelt passions, values, and beliefs; you usually have more fulfilling and satisfying experiences; and you are much more likely to achieve good and gratifying results.

Strata-Gem:

Before, during, and after *Crunch Time*, the healthiest course of action for you to take is to honestly identify and explore the motives behind your desires and decisions, and to make certain that they reflect your most heartfelt values and will help you to secure your most cherished goals.

OUT-OF-THE-BOX DECISION-MAKING, AND TRULY UNDERSTANDING THE INDIVIDUALS INVOLVED IN YOUR DECISIONS

In sports, you often hear coaches and managers say that they "play the percentages" when deciding how to compete most effectively against a given opponent. This generally means that if you know an opponent has a weakness, you exploit it. For example, if a batter on an opposing team loves to hit fastballs, but often can't hit a curveball, you throw him or her lots of curveballs. Similarly, if you know that your opponent's forehand is far better than his or her backhand, you serve to his or her backhand. In essence, by repeating something that has given you or someone else a successful outcome in the past you are increasing the percentage that you will secure a successful outcome again.

Sometimes, however, it is appropriate, wise, and constructive when making a decision to go against the percentages, do something different, and not play it safe.

For example, if the batter in the example above receives *only* curveballs, he or she can then begin to anticipate them and prepare for them; and if the batter has any talent at all, he or she can make an appropriate adjustment in his or her swing, thereby increasing the chances that he or she will get a hit—even if curves are a weakness. Similarly, if people keep serving to my backhand, which is my weaker stroke, I will just anticipate it and step around the serve and hit it with my forehand.

To my mind, the really smart opponent serves to my strength—my forehand—every once in a while, to keep me guessing, to surprise me, and to keep me from covering up my weaker stroke. Additionally, I won't get into a rhythm of hitting just backhand returns. It's the savvy opponent who decides to take the calculated risk of serving to my strengths in order to exploit my weakness more effectively in the long run.

In real-life decision-making, just as in sports, there are times to "play the percentages" and do what has worked in the past. However, there are also times when it is *appropriate* to do something creative and different, to shake up the status quo by doing something unanticipated. This we will call doing something "out of the box."

Out-of-the-Box decision-making at the *appropriate* time can be very effective and constructive. Effective *Crunch Time* decision-makers often either possess a great sense of when to change strategies, or else they are blessed with a great coach. Either way, being an appropriately creative decision-maker is an essential quality of being a great decision-maker, and is necessary if you wish to attain your most precious goals and dreams. Here are a few examples.

Before I was born, my mother was an artist, an interior decorator, and on her way to getting her graduate degree in psychology. When I was born, she decided to postpone the pursuit of her degree and end her interior decorating business. She believed that giving up her interior decorating might mean less money coming into our household, but that the development of my emotional security was vastly more important than the extra financial security. She devoted most of her time to raising me, and to this day I'm amazed by how much she knew about me and how this understanding helped me to develop and grow in many unanticipated ways.

For example, despite some major problems as a child, I developed a love of racket sports when I was about nine years old. Somehow, my mom sensed that if I became more athletic, improved my agility, and developed a skill, I would feel better about myself and things would begin to fall into place. There were many times when she chose to overlook the fact that I had not done my homework or that I had missed late-afternoon religious school so that I could play ball. There were even times when I would plead with my mom to let me stay home from elementary school, just so I could play paddle tennis. And every once in a while she would.

Somehow, my mom knew that I was crying out to be good at something. That something turned out to be racket sports. As I played, I began to take weight off, and I eventually kept it off. I also became more agile. Slowly, I began to experience and enjoy the gratifying feelings of mastery and growing self-esteem. And once I began to feel better about myself, I gradually developed the overall confidence to vigorously tackle and master other endeavors, such as schoolwork, hobbies, and subsequently, my professional life. I found that I loved doing things well. The rewards and recognition that I received were incredibly gratifying.

In the case of a parent such as my mom, who did something that wasn't exactly orthodox but was in the best interests of their child, I would call that act *Out-of-the-Box* decision-making. In my case, I *did* learn how to spell and read. I *did* learn how to write and add. And I am probably just as spiritual as many of the star students of my childhood religious school classes. So nothing of great consequence was lost in the process because my mom allowed me to miss a few school days or religious classes to pursue athletics. Yet *so* much was gained by my becoming an athlete—the benefits I took from my athletic experiences have had an immense impact on my overall development, in every facet of my life. By allowing me to pursue athletics in something of an unorthodox fashion, my mom made a calculated and understanding-based decision. She responded with flexibility and creativity to my unique situation, and that response was based upon her extraordinary knowledge of and intuition regarding my true needs.

I believe that one of the reasons I have been successful in some of my endeavors is that I have learned from the example that my mom set. I learned that there are indeed times when you have to be creative, to use your intimate knowledge of a situation, and to try something unorthodox in order to effect a desired result. In essence, you need to engage in *Out-of-the-Box* decision-making.

Another example of *Out-of-the-Box* decision-making occurred a little later in my life. At the age of fourteen, I began high school at Brooklyn Polytechnic Preparatory Country Day School, aka "Poly Prep." As I later realized, Poly would be one of the most rigorous and demanding academic experiences of my life. During my career there, my mark was made as the number-one player on the varsity tennis team and as an average student. Between being a "brain" or a "jock," I was definitely considered by all to be the latter. Throughout my life, starting with paddle tennis, athletics made me stand out from the crowd, and my life at Poly was no exception. During the fall of my freshman year, I tried out for the varsity tennis team and beat the reigning number-one player, who was a senior, 6–1, 6–0. Thanks to athletics, I was once again deemed "special." I became known and written about in the school newspaper as the "freshman phenom." As a result of all this positive reinforcement, my tennis continued to take precedence over my schoolwork—in a *big* way. The problem was that Poly prided itself on its academic stature and its reputation for getting a large number of students into Ivy League colleges.

An illustration of where my priorities stood occurred one afternoon during my sophomore year, in biology class. After class, I was to play a match against my toughest opponent of the year. The biology teacher had us looking at and dissecting flies all week—even the nerds in our class were bored out of their minds. As we stood around the microscope, my friends began asking me about my upcoming, all-important athletic encounter. When the teacher heard us talking, he stood up and sarcastically inquired, "Lindner, would you rather be out practicing for your match or learning biology?" (*Crunch Time* #1.) To his surprise, I instantly answered, "Mr. Crenshaw, do you want to know the truth?"

"Yes, by all means, Mr. Lindner. Tell us." I then made my stand.

"Okay. Today's match, sir, will decide who will be the number one player in New York City. I'd rather be out practicing for it." For an instant, he looked at me incredulously (probably for having the guts to tell the truth). He then yelled, in the most disdainful way possible, "Just get out of here!"

Although I did win the battle—I defeated my opponent that

afternoon—the overall war wasn't going as well, because I was summoned into the headmaster's office the next day to explain my disrespectful behavior in biology. I could tell by the way Mr. Smith talked down to me that he perceived me as one of those dumb jocks who wouldn't cut it academically or professionally, but who made Poly a well-rounded school. I was a necessary evil, of sorts. Within a couple of moments, the "talk" was over and I was sent back to class.

Every spring, we had our end-of-the-school-year academic and athletic awards ceremony. It was quite the gathering—parents, family, and alumni. In each of my first three years, I was given the "Most Valuable Tennis Player" award. All three years, the same Poly/Harvard alumnus, Mr. Howe, gave out the "Harvard Award" to the most academically accomplished member of the senior class. After the awards ceremony in my junior year Mr. Howe walked up to me and said, "Ken, I've seen you get the tennis award for the past three years. Have you ever considered going to Harvard?" Before I could answer, the headmaster, Mr. Smith (who was a Harvard alumnus), took me by the shoulders, and directed me away. When he walked back over to Mr. Howe, he said, "He's not Harvard material." Mr. Smith then introduced Mr. Howe to the class members whom he felt *were* "Harvard material."

I heard the headmaster's remark, and feelings of hurt and shame surged through me like a bolt of lightning. It was the same feeling that I had experienced as a child when I tried to buy candy at the diner and the owner embarrassed me in front of all the customers. I quickly left the post-ceremony gathering, to collect myself and protect whatever was left of my already minimal academic self-esteem.

During the first semester of my senior year, I took a psychology/sociology class, and I loved every minute of it. I actually began to do my homework. My teacher, Mr. Morrison, apparently saw something in me. He believed in me. He encouraged me. He expected the best from me. Academically, this experience proved to be a turning point in my life.

At about the same time, an older tennis friend, who was a Harvard recruiter, suggested that I apply to Harvard. Another recruiter called me about Columbia. When I later went to Mr. Smith and told him that I was planning to apply to Columbia, he laughed. When I delicately told him that I was also thinking about applying to Harvard, he became angry and said all-knowingly, "Don't waste Harvard's time and your money. You could never get in. Besides, I won't even write the recommendation that you'll need for your application to be considered." He then took me by the shoulders and quickly escorted me out of his office.

That evening, I went home and told my mom about my meeting with Mr. Smith. (*Crunch Time #2.*) She thought about the situation overnight and then decided that an *Out-of-the-Box* plan of attack was required. The next day, she arranged a meeting with Mr. Smith for the following week.

During that meeting, my mom presented Mr. Smith with a photograph of me as a fat child. She explained that I had been quite overweight and exceedingly awkward, and that athletics had helped me to develop physically and psychologically, and had added greatly to my self-confidence and positive outer and inner sense of identity. That both tennis and paddle tennis had in fact become an integral part of my life and were almost like crutches that I would need to be weaned from. My mom believed—and conveyed to Mr. Smith—that I was clearly growing and expanding academically. She cited the "As" that I was getting in my psychology/sociology class, as well as the high marks that I was starting to receive in my other classes. She told Mr. Smith that I had always been a late bloomer, and that I was just starting to blossom academically. Somehow my mom got through to him.

After confirming my mother's assertions with my various instructors, Mr. Smith agreed that if my grades continued to rise during that first semester of my senior year, he would write "some kind" of recommendation to Harvard for me—but to be sure, it would *not* be a good one. As the meeting ended, my mom thanked him for his courtesy and for keeping an open mind.

That evening, my mom explained the deal that she had made with Mr. Smith. Because of the confidence and mastery that I was gaining academically, I enjoyed keeping my end of the bargain. That semester, my grades rose substantially, and at the appropriate time, I handed Mr. Smith my Harvard recommendation form. I was told that he would keep his end of the bargain.

Because of my tennis successes and the fact that I was attending such a highly regarded school, there were a number of colleges that contacted me. I began to feel that I would be accepted into a good school and wouldn't have to take the basket-weaving courses that Mr. Smith had recommended the year before. I began to develop confidence about my academic future, because Columbia and the University of Pennsylvania were taking great pains to get me to consider coming to their schools. As it turned out, I needed all the confidence and *Out-of-the-Box* decision-making poise that I could muster for my two Harvard interviews.

My first Harvard interview took place at a stodgy Wall Street law firm. I had apparently arrived early, because the two interviewees who were scheduled before me arrived at the same time that I did. We were all asked to write down our grade-point averages, SAT scores, and academic awards. The male interviewee listed his A+ average, his combined SAT scores of 1530 (out of 1600), and his impressive Latin and writing awards. The female interviewee put down her A average, her 1580 college-board scores, and her perfect scores in the Latin and French achievement tests. She was also valedictorian of her class. I was next. I carefully sheltered everything that I wrote from the other two. I began to laugh while I scribbled, as I wasn't in their academic league. But, what the heck. It was a rainy afternoon and I had nothing better to do.

The interviewer, a Harvard alumnus, was running late, so we all sat in the austere waiting room trying not to stare at each other. I could tell that both the girl and the guy were as tight as drums. I could literally see their hands shaking.

Finally, the guy was called in. About ten minutes later, he came out looking totally dejected. After he got his raincoat from the closet, he threw it down and said, "I've been waiting all my life for this interview, and this pompous asshole spent five minutes with me and barely listened to anything I had to say. I'm *so* screwed!"

The girl looked at him and then at me as she took a big gulp of water. She was then escorted in. Almost as quickly as the guy, she came out with a glazed look in her eyes. I asked her how it went. She said that he seemed like he was in a really bad mood, and that she just knew that it didn't go well. She exited the room quickly.

I was now alone in the waiting room. I took a deep breath and thought to myself, "The one thing I know is that both of the people before me felt that the interviewer never gave them a chance, and they both left feeling that they—or he—blew it." At that moment; I was called in for my interview.

When I entered the interviewer's office, he was on the phone having a heated conversation with a junior associate. He was so angry that the veins in his neck had begun to bulge, and I began to wonder whether his tie might snap off. Finally, the phone conversation ended. He popped a couple of Tums into his mouth and did his best to compose himself. He introduced himself and told me that it had been a very long day. As he spoke, he looked on his desk for the academic information that I had jotted down upon arrival. After reviewing my academic background, he put the paper down. He had an irritated look, as if to say, "Why am I wasting my time here?" He then stared straight at me and said, "Why did you even *bother* applying to Harvard?" (*Crunch Time* #3.)

In an instant, I thought to myself that I wasn't going to let this guy eat me up the way he had the other two applicants. I looked squarely back at him, and with the most cavalier but sincere look and manner I could muster, replied, "Sir, I never even thought about applying to Harvard. I'm here only because Harvard asked *me* to apply. I know that I'm going to be accepted to Columbia and Penn. But because I'm the captain and the number-one player on the Eastern Junior Davis Cup Team and the number-one player in New York City, I was approached by members of your school."

Suddenly, something changed. His posture picked up. He smiled at me and said, "Please, tell me more about yourself." I then explained that I had never really focused on my academics until my senior year; but when you combine my B average at Poly Prep, my higher grades the past semester, and my tennis accomplishments, recruiters from schools such as Harvard, Penn, Princeton, and Columbia had been calling. We spoke for about an hour or so, as he asked me question after question about my academic and athletic backgrounds. At the end, we shook hands, and he said that he had enjoyed the meeting.

As I now reflect on this scenario, I believe that my *Out-of-the-Box* decision to turn the tables on him worked. I also believe that my career as an agent began on that January day.

My second Harvard interview took place in Cambridge, Massachusetts, on a crisp Saturday in February. My parents and I arrived on campus a little early, so we had plenty of time to walk around before my 11:00 A.M. meeting. As we strolled, I thought that Harvard was magnificent. Harvard Yard and Harvard Square radiated with tradition and timeless beauty. We visited the Harvard bookstore, and I felt inspired to read and learn as never before. The whole tour was a feast for the visual and cerebral senses. However, I didn't want to let myself enjoy anything too much, because I was sure there'd be no way that I'd be admitted there.

We arrived at Holyoke Center about fifteen minutes early for my meeting with Jeffrey Blackman, one of the head admissions officers. When Mr. Blackman came to get me, he shook my hand warmly and introduced himself as "Jeff." He then walked me to his office, stopping every few feet to point out Harvard landmarks through the large glass picture windows. It became clear that everything about this meeting would be in stark contrast to the first one.

Jeff immediately mentioned that he had played on the Harvard freshman tennis team, and that he was very impressed with all of my tennis achievements. He also took the initiative to say that he had studied my transcripts and that he was pleased to see the sharp rise in my grades during the first semester of my senior year. We then talked for close to an hour about my background—and his. By this time, I had been through a number of interviews with other college admissions people, and my meeting with Jeff was by far the most comfortable. He was a great guy and I felt that he took the time to get to know me well.

As we were finishing, I decided to express my appreciation, as well as to throw out some bait to see how the interview had gone. "Mr. Blackman," I said, "I just want to tell you that I know that I'm not going to get into Harvard, but I want to thank you for taking the time to truly listen to and understand me."

Then the most surprising thing happened. He said, with conviction, "On the contrary, I think you've got a *great* chance to be accepted here. Your tennis and paddle tennis achievements are extraordinary. You come from a great school and you're now showing that you can more than handle Poly's workload." Suddenly, the most incredible adrenaline rush shot through my body. I had a chance!

He continued, "I just don't understand why more well-rounded people such as yourself don't apply here." With that statement, I saw and seized my opportunity. (*Crunch Time* #4.) I immediately replied, "I know why." "Then please tell me," he said with the greatest of interest. I explained to him that when I had approached my headmaster about applying to Harvard, he had become angry and told me not to even bother wasting Harvard's time and my money, that I'd never get in. I could see Jeff growing upset. So I continued, "Mr. Smith then said that he would refuse to even write a recommendation for me, so that my application wouldn't ever get processed." By this time, Jeff was clearly angry. (*Crunch Time* #5.) I pressed on. "Were it not for my mom having explained my situation to Mr. Smith, and finally getting him to agree that, if my grades rose substantially, he would write some type of recommendation, I couldn't and wouldn't have applied. And I'm as sure as I can be that whatever Mr. Smith *did* write wasn't positive, and that he strongly recommended that I not be considered for admission to Harvard."

A second later, Jeff thumbed through my admissions file, found Mr. Smith's letter, and read it to see if it confirmed all that I had recounted. He then held the recommendation up and proceeded to toss it into the wastebasket. As he did this, he said passionately and emphatically, "That's what I think of Mr. Smith and others like him." Jeff then stood up and said, "Ken, just so you know, I feel very good about you and our meeting."

On April 14, one day before everyone received their college

admission letters of acceptance or rejection, I received a call from Columbia. I had been accepted. I was happy and relieved, but my heart was with Harvard.

The next day, the top two students at Poly were accepted to Harvard. However, the number-three student, who was the editor of our newspaper and who had worked his whole high school career for a Harvard admission, was rejected. (Thankfully, he was accepted at Yale.)

That morning, all I could think about was Harvard. I felt that there were others who unquestionably deserved to go there more than I, but I knew that if given the chance, I would make the most of it and appreciate it forever.

At about 10:30, an assistant from the front office came to get me out of math class, and handed me a note to call home. I knew this was it. My heart pounded. My hands shook. I was short of breath. I had no right to expect a "yes," but I wanted it more than anything in my life.

I dialed our number. It rang twice. My mom picked up. Laughing with happiness, she said, "You got in! You got into Harvard!!!"

For a moment, I was in nirvana. I jumped up and yelled, "Yes!", attracting the attention of everyone in the front office. Chills ran through me. I asked my mom to read the acceptance letter to me—three times. I thanked her for being the best mother ever. Since my dad was in Europe on business, she was going to call him and send a telegram. It was a moment that I will never, ever forget.

I knew that my next move was to see Mr. Smith. April 15 was always a big day for Poly, and Mr. Smith was kept abreast of who did and didn't get accepted into which colleges. He already knew through the grapevine that out of the top ten students in our class, only two had been accepted at Harvard. He also had been told that I had been accepted to Columbia the day before.

As I was escorted into Mr. Smith's office, I was doing all that I could to contain my smile and exuberance. Inside, though, I was *bursting*.

He took one look at me and his eyes widened. He realized that his greatest fear had come to pass. I had been accepted to *his* alma mater. He began to stutter as he inquired, "Y-Y-You got in?" I smiled warmly and acted as calmly as I could as I told him the good news. He looked down to the floor, and for a long moment, he was at a loss for words.

I understood how he felt. From his vantage point, there were others who deserved to be accepted far more than I did—if academic accomplishment over the course of a high school career was the sole admissions criterion. In order to fill the gap of silence, I said, "Mr. Smith, I know that others may deserve to be accepted to Harvard more than I do, but I won't let you or Poly down. And I do appreciate your keeping an open mind about writing my recommendation to Harvard."

He then said, in as optimistic a tone as he could muster, "I *think* you'll be all right. Just remember, you have been given a special opportunity that thousands upon thousands of young people your age dream about. Use it wisely."

"Thank you, sir, I will," I said as he shook my hand.

Within an hour, my news had spread throughout Poly. When I walked into the cafeteria, people stood up and cheered. I guess my acceptance to Harvard represented a victory for the proletariat and the downtrodden, as well as for the many students whom Mr. Smith had similarly dissuaded from applying to their dream schools. As I walked through the massive lunchroom, people were yelling, shaking my hand, and patting me on the back. I felt like Richard Gere in the closing scene of *An Officer and a Gentleman*, as he carried Debra Winger out of the factory to the cheers and smiles of her coworkers.

During my first year at Harvard, I made the freshman Dean's List and, similar to my career at Poly, I defeated the number-one player on the varsity tennis team in a practice match within a few days of my arrival there. After the school year ended and I returned to Brooklyn, I called Mr. Smith to set up an appointment to see him. At that meeting, I shared the good news with him. He was happy and we began to bond. He realized that what my mom had told him a year or so earlier had been true.

Three years later, I called Mr. Smith to tell him that I was going to graduate Harvard magna cum laude. I also shared my tennis successes with him. He told me that my call was fortuitous, because Mr. Howe, who had given out the Harvard Cup for eight years in a row, had just called to say that he couldn't make it that year. Amazingly, Mr. Smith said, "Kenny, I can't think of anyone more suited than you to give out the Harvard Cup this year." My insides swelled up with a kind of love, gratitude, and validation that can't be put into words. Needless to say, I felt great about his offer and accepted the invitation.

Ironically, after the awards ceremony was over, Mr. Smith and I stood in the exact same place where Mr. Howe and I had stood five years earlier, when Mr. Smith had escorted me away, saying that I wasn't "Harvard material." Mr. Smith then took me aside and said, "Kenny, even though I'm going to retire this year, one is never too old to learn. You and your mom taught me a great lesson: Never prejudge anyone. I thought I knew you—but I didn't. I thought I saw who you were, but *eyesight doesn't mean insight*. I never thought you were capable of doing as well as you have. From this example, I've learned to keep an open mind and to see beyond what's apparent. You should thank your mom, because were it not for her faith in you and her understanding of you, I never would have written any recommendation for you. She's very special."

As he spoke, tears welled up in my eyes.

In parting, he smiled and said, "You know, you're a legend at Poly. Now students from the bottom quarter of the class apply to Harvard and Yale and say, 'If Lindner can do it, why can't I?' In fact, just the other day, one of our top students complained, 'Because of Lindner, any idiot thinks that, with a little luck, he can get into Harvard.'"

We exchanged the warmest of smiles, a hug, and a long handshake before parting.

One more *Out-of-the-Box* decision. Years ago, our company took on the representation of a prospective client—not from a demo tape, as was our usual practice, but as a result of a captivating commercial picture, a stellar resume, and a wonderful in-person meeting. It was at that meeting that the extraordinary sparkle, passion, and wisdom in that prospective client's eyes and soul mirrored those qualities found in her head shot. Her very impressive background included graduating Phi Beta Kappa from a fine university, being an All-American college basketball player, winning the Miss U.S.A. Junior Miss title, and possessing a thorough knowledge of basketball and other sports.

Two of this talented woman's goals were to become a major network sports broadcaster and to have a major role in a program such as *Entertainment Tonight*. Within a few weeks of our association, an on-air position at Movie Time, the forerunner of today's E! Network opened up. She tested for it and got it. From that position, she gained some on-air experience and a much more polished demo tape with which we could market her.

A number of months later, a major sports opportunity opened up for a woman at NBC. We were told that the prerequisites for the job were being a "breakthrough" talent, and having prior local, cable, and/or network sports experience. Notwithstanding the requirements of a prior sports broadcasting background, we sent our client's tape for consideration. The network's response was: "She's got the talent, but how can we hire someone with no sports broadcasting experience for this job? Thanks, but no thanks."

The orthodox route of submitting our client's tape didn't work. It was time for an *Out-of-the-Box* approach. I took a day or so to think things through. My associate and I knew that our client had a thorough knowledge of sports. She just needed the opportunity to show it to the appropriate individuals. Unfortunately, the person who would ultimately make the decision didn't think that a meeting with our client would be worthwhile. This was coupled with the fact that he was someone with whom we had no prior history or working relationship. But we decided to try my plan anyway.

I called the network executive and identified all of the on-air individuals whom I had "discovered" and brought to his and other networks, in an attempt to establish my credibility with him. Before I finished giving my full list, he acknowledged my very good eye for spotting breakthrough talent. I then said that we were positive that if he were to have a one-on-one meeting with our client (who was based in Los Angeles—he was in New York), she would win him over with her sports knowledge. I told him that I would bet my credibility and my future relationship with him on it. I then offered to send him a first-class, round-trip ticket to Los Angeles and put him up in his fa-vorite L.A. hotel if he would sit down and have a meal with her. Our deal would be: If he didn't hire our client, I've paid for everything. If he did like her, I'd be reimbursed.

I could tell by his reaction that I'd gotten him to seriously ac-knowledge my strong belief in our client. The unorthodox nature and novelty of the approach worked. He said, "Kenny I can't accept your proposal, although I do like the effort. But here's what we can do. I'm going to be in Phoenix next week. How about having your client fly down to meet me there?"

I instantly accepted the offer, and once again reassured him of my client's thorough sports knowledge. The next week they met. Three days later, she was offered the job. As a result, an exhilarating and en-forcing come-from-behind victory was secured for our client.

Two factors played major roles here. One was that we knew our client and her abilities well, and we understood that if she met this guy in person, she'd dazzle him with her basketball knowledge and great presence. Two, we needed to step back, get another perspective, and find a more unorthodox and creative approach that would shake up the unfavorable status quo. In this instance, we found it.

Effective *Out-of-the-Box* decision-making can be a real kick and in-credibly rewarding.

Strata-Gems:

- There are times in life when orthodox strategies and behav-ior are not the most effective or constructive ones. In some in-stances, deciding to create a new and/or an unorthodox strategy may be the most appropriate and efficacious means of achieving your goals.

- Having a true understanding of someone is a very important component of reaching a wise decision regarding that individual.

- Eyesight doesn't necessarily mean insight.

GETTING IT RIGHT—FROM THE START

This book is based upon the premise that it's *never* too late to change, to grow, and to become a wiser decision-maker. On the other hand, some of the best advice that I can share with my clients is that when starting a new job, or beginning a new professional relationship, do your best to get it right—the first time around. As a society, we often base our opinions on our first impressions. And it frequently takes a great deal to change our minds, when and if individuals or events happen to get off to a bad or a lackluster start. In some cases, we may never change someone's first perceptions . . . even if these perceptions are totally inaccurate.

Beginning with my childhood, and to this day, I am one of those individuals whom people often underrate. Therefore, if and when I succeed, people are surprised. In fact, just a few weeks ago, I played a series of sets against the head pro of a well-known resort, and beat him in a number of them. Apparently, later on, a few guests walked up to the pro and commented that they couldn't understand how I had fared so well against him. They just didn't get it.

The pro responded, "Kenny's deceptive! You don't get it until you play him." The other pro, against whom I had also played some sets, then added, "I said the same thing when I first saw him. Then I played him. He is *really* good. We call him, 'The Deceptor,' because his playing deceives everybody."

Being underrated, possibly because I've been a late bloomer in many things, is something that I've experienced throughout my life. I've learned to understand it and to deal with it. However, I have also experienced the great advantages that can be derived from getting it right and earning people's respect from the get go. For example, it's much easier to be highly seeded (ranked) in a big tournament—you get right into the main draw; you may not have to play a match until the second round; and you may not play another top-ranked player until the later rounds. This is in sharp contrast to having to play through three or four qualifying rounds just to get into the main tournament, and then, if you make it, possibly having to play a top-seeded player such as Andre Agassi in the first round. If I am going to play an Andre Agassi, I'd much rather do it in the finals of a tournament than in the first round.

During my freshman year of high school, I signed up to try out for the varsity tennis team. I told the coach about my paddle tennis successes, and he scheduled me to play a match the following week against the returning number-one varsity player, who was also the team captain. I knew that this match would be my shot to get off on the right track. It would be my defining moment—my *Crunch Time*—to show that I belonged on the varsity team. During the intervening days, I practiced and mentally prepared. I wound up beating my opponent 6–1, 6–0 in about fifty minutes. For the next four years, I was automatically given the number-one spot on the varsity team, and I never again had to play another challenge match against any of my teammates. The perception—true or false—was that I was the best player on the team, and that no one was going to beat me. So as a result of my first and only inter-team match, the case was *closed*—I would play number-one singles.

In college, the same thing happened. On my first day at the tennis courts during my freshman year, I was introduced to the number-one player (a senior) on the varsity team. He was waiting until the other team members arrived so that he could practice with them. After a moment or two, the varsity coach suggested that the number-one player and I play a quick set. As the coach had never seen me play before,

I once again knew that this could be a big *Crunch Time* opportunity for me. I quickly decided to use the *Strategy* of focusing as best I could on executing each stroke to the best of my ability. This *Strategy* worked and I played as well as I was capable of. I won the set, 6–3. We played another. I won it, 6–2. By now, a number of varsity team members were watching, along with a now amused and excited coach. We played once more. I won, 6–4. Although according to Ivy League rules I had to play on the freshman tennis team, my situation immediately and materially changed as a result of that fateful match. From then on, I was extended the privilege of practicing with the varsity, along with attending separate practice sessions with my freshman teammates. The keener competition that I faced at the varsity level helped me remain undefeated in inter-school match play my freshman year.

A few months after I began my career at the William Morris Agency, I was given the important assignment of writing all of the contracts and being the agency's business affairs point-person for the new morning *David Letterman Show*. This program would make William Morris a good deal of money in commissions. Upon receiving this assignment, like the high school and college tennis matches discussed above, I knew that this would be a defining moment (*yes, Crunch Time*) for me with my new employers. With this in mind, I busted my butt, spending late evening and weekend time making my very best effort, right from the start. The work paid off. David's managers were so pleased that one of them, Jack Rollins, sent a letter to one of the heads of William Morris detailing how happy he and his client, David, were with my meticulousness, the amount of responsibility that I had assumed, and how well I interacted with the show's staff members. All of this allowed my career to get off to a very positive and visible start, and I was immediately accorded respect for my efforts and for my effectiveness.

Conversely, if you recall from the previous section, I didn't initially focus on my schoolwork at Poly Prep. As a result, I was perceived by many as someone who wasn't very bright. And some individuals, such as my senior English teacher, could never get over their first impressions of me as strictly a dumb jock. Had these particular impressions been given greater weight, they could have easily influenced my headmaster to ultimately decide not to write *any* Harvard recommendation for me.

In the broadcasting arena, I have a number of special/unusual clients who have been fortunate enough, relative to their early stages of development, to begin their careers in markets that are large and advanced. Often, this occurs when individuals begin as interns, writers, or producers in their hometown or college markets and work themselves up through the ranks to on-air positions at stations there. Since these individuals didn't have to start out in the usual small-market setting, where they could make their expected and accepted rookie on-air mistakes, they wind up making them in large markets where others are much more seasoned and polished. Therefore, their mistakes are greatly magnified—and are tolerated a great deal less. One problem with this situation is that news management at these stations will forever—or at least for a long time thereafter—have those rookie mistakes in the backs of their minds, and these managers are often never able to objectively see and acknowledge the subsequent growth of these people. This reality is reflected in the fact that these individuals continually make lower salaries and are promoted at a slower rate. The first impressions that they make as rookies, and the perception that they're being given a break by being allowed to start their on-air careers in large markets, generally stay with these managers throughout these newscasters' tenures at these stations. As a result, these newscasters are often forced to leave their first stations, even if they ordinarily would have been happy to stay there. They instead must go on to stations where management's first impression of them is a positive one and accurately reflects their advanced stage of development.

But I've saved the worst first-impression story for last . . .

I remember my first paid summer position at a law firm, which I held in the months between my second and third years of law school. As I had no prior real law practice experience, there were many issues and nuances that I just didn't get. And my peers either *did* get them, or they hid their befuddlement better than I did.

One Friday afternoon at about five o'clock, about two weeks after I started there, I was called into a meeting with the senior partner. As I entered his office, it appeared as if he had just gone through a very heated meeting with a client over a potential snag in their case. As I sat there, he yelled and screamed at his secretary, his associates, and everyone else within range. After a few very tense and uncomfortable minutes, the partner told me that he was in a rush, and that he had to present me with an important question regarding his case before he took off for the weekend. He needed the answer *first thing* Monday morning, because his client would be coming back to discuss strategy at 10:00 A.M. that day.

I was all ready to dazzle him. I would work throughout the weekend to have his answer and a strategy mapped out for him on Monday. I was set with my pen and yellow legal pad when he laid the bomb on me. It was a *bankruptcy* problem, I knew *absolutely nothing* about bankruptcy, because it was a third-year law school course.

I started to explain that I hadn't taken bankruptcy yet. Half listening, he said, "Aw, don't sweat it, you can do it." He then proceeded to spew out the facts of the case in language that I couldn't for the life of me make heads or tails of.

As I began to ask him to explain some of it to me in more detail, he said that he had to run and would see me on Monday. When I tried, once again, to get him to further clarify the problem, he looked at me as if he would kill me if I uttered another word. His secretary, sensing another ugly eruption, hastily escorted me out the door.

After I left his office, I read my notes. Egyptian hieroglyphics would have made more sense to me. I went downstairs and cornered the firm's bankruptcy expert, and asked him to explain what I had written down. After reading my gibberish, he looked at me as if I were speaking another language, and said, "I don't know what the hell you've got there, Ken. Good luck." I struggled all weekend, but I couldn't figure out the facts or the problem. On Monday morning, I arrived at the partner's office at 9:00 A.M. Looking much more relaxed than he did on Friday afternoon, he calmly asked, "OK, what's the answer?"

In the most sincere manner I could muster, I responded, "What's the question?"

Suddenly, I saw the veins bulge in his neck, and his quickly reddening face took on a terribly contorted look.

After a moment or two of trying in vain to control what was well-known to be an ugly temper, he yelled, "What the hell do you mean, 'What's the question?' My client's coming in an hour and I need answers!"

I calmly replied, "I don't take bankruptcy until my third year, Mr. Baumgartner, and I didn't understand the problem you gave me on Friday. And no one downstairs could figure it out, either."

With a bloodcurdling scream, he yelled to his secretary to "Cancel the 10:00 A.M. meeting with Kreiger. Tell him I'm sick. *Really sick!*" He then looked at me as if he were ready to take my heart out of my chest with his bare hands.

Luckily, he just told me to leave. Within an hour, the story had spread throughout the firm. You want to talk about a bad, irreversible start. This was it.

After that, no one had confidence in me, and as a result, I began to lose confidence in myself. Eventually I didn't care enough to prove anyone wrong. The law firm's partners' and associates' poor perception of me became a reality.

As many others have learned by experience, when people expect the best from you and believe in you, these feelings and their positive energy often inspire you to perform at a higher level. Some of the coaches for whom I played in the past unconditionally believed in me. They never expected me to lose. Unquestionably, I played my best for them. *When counseling my clients, I am acutely aware of how very important it is for them to work for people who believe in them, are excited about them, and want to enhance them.* I also know that these employers will be much more likely to continue to do good things for my clients, if my clients make a good first impression. It's just a fact of life.

Strata Gem:

When making decisions, remember that whatever course of action you choose to take, first impressions are important. As a result, you will be well-served to focus on being prepared and doing constructive, enhancing, and appropriate things right from the start.

DON'T BE AFRAID TO TRY

When counseling individuals, I have encountered on more occasions than I can remember instances where they were either afraid to articulate their *Heart-of-Heart's* desire, or were afraid to put themselves on the line and go after it. They feared the embarrassment, disappointment, and pain of failure. Whenever this scenario comes up, I recount an incident that, more than any other, positively changed my life.

When I was a junior in high school, I took a public bus as part of my daily transportation to and from school. About twice a week, upon getting on the bus, I would see the most beautiful girl I had ever laid eyes on. Every time I'd see her, my heart would pound harder and faster. She literally took my breath away. The paralyzing problem was that I was much too shy and insecure to go up to her, even though we often made eye contact and she, more than once, smiled at me.

I rationalized my passivity by thinking that someone as beautiful as she would never be interested in me. She also looked older than I was, so I'd convince myself that she wouldn't be interested in someone younger. Then, one spring day, I saw her at my beach club, surrounded by a bunch of twenty-three- and twenty-four-year-old lifeguards and other "older" guys. My rationalizations for not approaching her were reinforced by this reality. I thought to myself, *She'd never be interested in me, so why bother trying?* Throughout the rest of the semester, I saw her on the bus. I thought about her constantly, but did nothing about it. The school year ended, and although that girl would remain in my thoughts long thereafter, I never saw her again. . . .

Then one day, about six years later, I had just graduated from college and was running my tennis instruction business. It was a Tuesday morning and I was at an indoor tennis complex, greeting some new students before they went onto the courts. At one point, I looked up and saw a woman enter the room. She was wheeling a carriage that contained a set of twin boys. Our eyes locked. My heart thumped. I felt chills along my spine. It was *her!!*

She came toward me. I walked to her. We both smiled. I quickly said, "I remember you!"

She said, "And I remember *you*! You were the guy who used to sit and stare at me on the bus."

I could feel the blood rush to my face. Smiling from ear to ear, I replied, "Yep, that was me."

She continued, "You know, I *always* wished you would have come up to me, because I was too shy to go up to you."

What a revelation! I was blown away. I thought to myself, *Did I just hear what I thought I heard?* So I asked, "Did you just say that you *wanted* me to come up and talk to you?!" She smiled and said, "I *always* did. Didn't you ever notice me smiling at you?"

I had to go on and ask, "If I had asked you out to dinner, would you have gone?" Smiling warmly and with great animation, she answered, "I absolutely would have! It's so funny to think about it now, but before you'd get on the bus, I used to think about what I'd say if you ever *did* come over and talk to me."

This was all astounding to me. The girl whom I'd dreamt about and whom I was too afraid to go up to had been hoping to go out with me all along!

I later learned that my fantasy woman's name was Barbara, and that she was married and loved being a mom to her two boys. Obviously, I had missed my golden opportunity years earlier because of my unfounded fear of being rejected and my overall feelings of insecurity.

The life lesson that I learned was: Don't be afraid to put yourself "on the line" and go after your dreams. To paraphrase President Franklin D. Roosevelt, "All you have to fear is fear itself." If you take the shot, you may attain your goal, and the worst that can happen is that you don't succeed this time around. Big deal! But as I learned from my "Barbara experience," even if I don't succeed, I can learn from the experience and become wiser and better equipped to succeed the next time.

In his book *Unlimited Power*, Anthony Robbins gives a list of how many defeats Abraham Lincoln suffered before he accomplished his lofty goal of becoming President:

1) Failed in business at age twenty-one.
2) Was defeated in a legislative race at age twenty-two.
3) Failed again in business at age twenty-four.
4) Overcame the death of his sweetheart at age twenty-six.
5) Had a nervous breakdown at age twenty-seven.
6) Lost a congressional race at age thirty-four.
7) Lost a congressional race at age thirty-six.
8) Lost a senatorial race at age forty-five.
9) Failed in an effort to become Vice President at age forty-seven.
10) Lost a senatorial race at age forty-nine.
11) Was elected President of the United States at age fifty-two.

What we can learn from this list is that everyone suffers defeats along the way toward accomplishing goals—even legends. In baseball, if you don't get up to bat, you can't get a hit, and even the best hitters only get hits about three out of every ten times that they try. We all fail. But some of us will never have the chance to win, because we'll never give ourselves the opportunity to secure a victory . . . *for fear of losing*.

The "Barbara experience" taught me that what's sad isn't failing to succeed. It's failing to try! People who lose the weight, or get the client, the job, "the order," the "girl," or the "guy"—know this. They try. They're proactive. They enter the race and put themselves in the best position to win. Their constructive decisions to "take a shot" are their vehicles.

Strata-Gem:

When it's appropriate, *don't be afraid to try!* This is a constructive decision that achievers and successful individuals learn how to make.

LONG-TERM DECISION-MAKING AND
THE POTENTIAL POISONS OF
POSITIVE REINFORCEMENT

Positive reinforcement, compliments, accolades, applause, respect, acknowledgment—all have been crucial to my development. They have moved, impelled, and catalyzed me to do many constructive and healthy things in my life, especially learning to be disciplined and to delay gratification. Early on, I recognized that discipline and delayed gratification were integral ingredients of my *Strategies* for success. Accepting this fact led and helped me to stay focused on my long-term goals, and to develop solid, well-thought-out, long-term game plans in order to achieve these goals. Positive reinforcement has fueled me with the passion and desire to lose weight, keep it off, and accomplish many of my most cherished goals in sports, academia, and business.

But often, the superficial roar of the crowd, the complimentary handshakes, and all of the positive attention can be intoxicating, addicting, dangerous, and *poisonous*. As I've often counseled my clients, these very things can and frequently do cause irreparable injury when they inadvertently and materially influence decisions.

For example, as much as positive reinforcement helped and inspired me to grow as a tennis player, it also at times retarded my development—so much so that I never grew to be the top-caliber player that I might have been. This I know for a fact. I impart this lesson and the following story, on a regular basis, to my clients.

Between the ages of fourteen and seventeen, I had a dominating forehand, which I developed during my years playing paddle tennis.

Because the paddle tennis court is so much smaller than a tennis court, I was able to hit almost all forehands, and thereby win just about all of my paddle tennis matches playing that way. In tennis—probably too many times—my strong forehand, my competitiveness, and my tenacity were enough to secure a victory, especially when I competed in local and East Coast tournaments.

During those years, it was commonplace for tennis players and spectators alike to admire and occasionally rave about how potent my forehand was. And since winning was so important to me, to my psyche, and to my fragile self-image, I would use only the tools during tournaments and practice with which I thought I could win. The problem was, I chose to rely so much on my strengths, such as my forehand, that I didn't focus on building up the lesser parts of my game, such as my backhand.

Eventually, my narrow, win-today mind-set cost me dearly, and permanently. When I needed a more well-rounded game, so that I could win on a more consistent basis against the top nationally ranked players, I often didn't have it. I had neglected to work on improving the weaker elements of my game in exchange for the immediate gratification and glory of winning now, and for all of the positive reinforcement and fun stuff that came with it.

In hindsight, in a more perfect world, some wise individual would have taken me aside and said, "Kenny, win a little less in high school and practice matches by working on the things you're not so good at. Don't be afraid to lose. Lay a solid, balanced, long-term foundation for yourself. Forgo some of the positive reinforcement you'll receive by always winning today. If you do, you'll be a more complete and better player in the long run, and you'll be better equipped to successfully compete and win at the highest levels of tennis tomorrow."

And, in a more perfect world, I would have been wise enough to listen and then make the constructive decision to follow that advice.

I can't change the past, and I can't bring back my youth, but I can be sensitive to and wary of the pitfalls of immediate gratification and quick-fix positive reinforcement (at the wrong time and place) when reaching my decisions. You can, too.

In some ways, positive reinforcement is much like a drug or alcohol—for a period of time it can mask a problem. Take a medication such as cortisone, for example. It can mask pain, but there's an inherent problem. Athletes who take cortisone feel better, and as a result will often play while injured. This can result in their not focusing on, correcting, or healing the cause of the pain, because the symptoms aren't as noticeable. This can—and frequently does—result in the exacerbation of the original injury. What can be even worse, I've been told, is that if one takes too much cortisone, it can cause severe internal damage beyond the injury that it masks.

A way for you to remember this lesson is to think about the situation in which strikingly good-looking men and women often have their outer beauty positively and excessively reinforced to the exclusion of their other qualities. I've seen so many instances where beautiful children will incessantly have only their appearance positively reinforced. Like winning, beauty is coveted by our society. However, I've also seen the grave problems that can result if a handsome male or beautiful female becomes inextricably and exclusively defined by their appearance, because their feelings of self-worth become continually tied to their good looks.

Because popularity, dates, and other attractive opportunities frequently come more easily to good-looking people, these individuals may not feel the need to develop other even more important and essential long-term qualities, such as intellect, personality, character, a sense of humor, discipline, sensitivity, persistence, etc. Why should they? Everything and everyone seems to come to them anyway, right?

Yes, but not necessarily forever.

What happens when the looks fade? What happens when the good-looking individuals are competing with those just as physically attractive, but who *also* have developed other qualities and strong emotional and cerebral skills? (An analogous situation to my forehand and backhand in tennis.)

What happens when the attractive men and women have to negotiate through real-life situations in which extraordinary looks aren't a factor in the equation? What happens in situations in which these individuals need to rely on life-coping mechanisms, such as their ability to reason clearly and to solve problems effectively?

They often come up empty.

The outcome for these beautiful people, who are flooded with positive reinforcement solely in regard to their exteriors, can be quite sad. Generally, they don't see the dangers of being intoxicated, because they are blinded by the excessive positive reinforcement; as a result, they evolve into extremely frustrated, puzzled, unbalanced, unhappy people, with their true potentials left undeveloped. Just like my full potential in tennis!

Never was this more clear than when a dinner guest shared a story with me about her ex-husband, who had been the big man on campus during his college days. While at school, he had striking good looks and was the quarterback of the varsity football team. He was the golden boy. However, after college graduation, he drifted—badly. Somehow, things didn't come as easily to him in the working world as they had in school. According to his ex-wife, when he finally landed a position as an insurance salesman and failed to excel there, he became bewildered. And after losing a number of potential clients to rival salesmen, he came home one night frustrated and angry. At dinner, when his then-wife tried to discuss the problem with him, he confided with great sadness, "I just don't understand why it's not working. I'm better looking than all those other sales guys! I just don't get it."

He was right. He didn't get it, or see it. He couldn't. He was still intoxicated with the positive reinforcement that he'd received years earlier, and he hadn't developed the inner goods that would buoy him in the long run. He never grew.

Conversely, years ago, a truly beautiful aspiring actress came into my office for a meeting. After talking with her, I was very impressed with how centered and value-based she was, as well as with the well-thought-out manner in which she viewed and lived her life. She was extremely wise. I was even more appreciative of her qualities in light of her beauty. As we continued to talk, I learned that she was a late bloomer, and that her looks hadn't been an asset until she reached the age of eighteen or so. She related that as a young girl, her parents had encouraged her to develop her other qualities. Her inner qualities. She had obviously chosen to heed their advice.

This woman was indeed fortunate—she wasn't intoxicated with positive reinforcement early on because her good looks didn't come to the fore until later. But here's an important point: *Constructive decision-makers can't always depend on fate or others to help them see past the mask of positive reinforcement.* Beware: Don't be taken in by the roar of the crowd and spectator accolades, or by what's easier or the most fun to attain. Once again, appropriate focus, discipline, and delayed gratification are the keys to success here.

It's nice to receive compliments—but not at the expense of being distracted from what's best for your continued growth and development in the long run, or what you truly, in your *Heart-of-Hearts*, desire.

Always remember: *Positive reinforcement isn't always positive!*

Strata-Gems:

• Positive reinforcement, when valid and accepted in the right situation, can be healthy and can help you to develop deserved high self-esteem. It can also fuel you with enough focus and discipline to allow you to accomplish your most cherished goals. However, it can also be intoxicating and harmful. If, through your decisions, you choose to do things aimed at eliciting more and more positive reinforcement, especially at the expense of ignoring those things that you need to do and to master in order for you to continue to grow, you will pay a price.

• Don't be afraid to experiment and try something new, if the hoped-for result of your experimentation will enhance you. If you take a misstep, or fail initially or repeatedly, don't be concerned about not receiving positive reinforcement, or about receiving negative reinforcement. Have courage and faith! The eventual accomplishment of your goal will bring you gratifying and valid inner positive reinforcement and feelings of high self-esteem.

THE EXPERIENCE AND ILLUSION
OF WINNING AND LOSING

"If you can meet with Triumph and Disaster,
*and treat those two impostors just the same . . . "**
Rudyard Kipling

As a kid, I hated—in fact, absolutely *detested*—losing. Especially on the paddle tennis court. Because winning was so much a part of my self-identity and over-all confidence, and because I felt that my public acceptability and popularity were directly tied to my athletic prowess, losing cut at my very core. In fact, early on in my paddle tennis career, my on-court demeanor made John McEnroe look like Miss Manners. That's no easy task, I assure you. If I started losing, my blood would boil. If it continued, I'd throw my paddle against the fence with as much venom and force as I could muster. Not a pretty sight. It is in this context of my burning need to win, all the time, that I'd go into my room during the next three years and reflect upon the following experiences. (Post–*Crunch Time* decision-making.)

At sixteen, I had become a successful East Coast junior tennis player. During that year, I entered a New York City men's tennis tournament. After defeating a couple of relatively weak opponents, I was

*This sage advice can be found at the entrance to the All-England Tennis Club, where Wimbledon is held.

pitted against a thirty-seven-year-old, top-ranked East Coast player. He was left-handed and had a wicked serve that spun off the court in a manner that was totally opposite from that of a right-hander.

I had never competed against a really talented left-handed player before. The problem was not only that his shots and spin were coming from different angles, but every time I expected to approach the net on his weaker backhand, I wound up approaching on his excellent forehand instead. I'd forget that he was a lefty. I was all crossed up.

He trounced me, 6–1, 6–1. What was worse, he confounded me. I seemed to be lost as to how to beat him.

After the match, and for a few days thereafter, I was emotionally blown away. My mom put things in perspective by helping me see the *Big Picture* of what had happened and what needed to be done. She observed that I had never played such a good and polished left-handed player before, and that I needed to learn how to play, and to be able to adjust my game to left-handers. We then decided to find a left-handed tennis coach to teach me, which turned out to be a very constructive decision.

We found a great coach who explained things in a manner that I could understand and implement. After about a year of practice, hard work, and improvement, I came up against that same left-handed opponent again. With a different perspective on things, better footwork, and a more complete arsenal of weapons, I defeated him fairly decisively, 6–3, 6–2. More importantly, I no longer had trouble adjusting to left-handed players.

After the match, I reflected on the fact that the loss to the left-hander a year earlier had seemed devastating when it happened. But I now realized that it identified a glaring flaw in my game that needed to be fixed. That devastating loss had triggered a positive and very necessary corrective decision and action. Now I was lying in bed, feeling great about my day's victory. My loss was really my first step toward developing a better all-around game and winning. Pretty interesting!

That same year, as a junior in high school, I competed in a tournament at Columbia University that featured the best high school players in the New York metropolitan area. The tournament was important not only for the collection of players it attracted, but because many top college recruiters used it as a means to scout talent.

I reached the finals, where I was to play against the tournament's top-seeded player. The match was to be played at 4:00 P.M. That day, I attended all of my classes and left school at 2:30. My mom drove me and my dad to the tournament. It turned out to be a seventy-five-minute trip. By the time I arrived at the tennis facility, it was almost four. My opponent was there waiting for me. I took the court, warmed up for about ten minutes, and we began to play. Or at least my opponent did.

Right from the beginning of the match, I felt stiff. Nothing flowed. My opponent, who had arrived at the facility at about 2:45 that day and had warmed up for about twenty minutes or so, jumped off to a fast start . . . and I never challenged him. I probably played one of the worst matches of my life. I was flat in every way. Physically. Mentally. You name it. I lost 6–1, 6–0. It was a disaster. Words can't explain how embarrassed I was in front of all of the college recruiters. It was brutal!

A couple of nights later, after some of the miserable sting from the loss had started to dissipate, I realized that I hadn't been mentally or physically ready to play the match.

I decided that from then on, I would make it my business to arrive at the tournament site at least an hour before my matches, so that I could hit some balls and get used to the surroundings, as well as stretch and mentally focus on the upcoming challenge. Next year, I'd skip classes before my big matches. I could always read someone's notes. You often only get one chance to win a big tournament. If I was going to make this kind of an investment in my tennis, I had to give myself *every* chance to win. *I had to seize the moment.*

The following year, after attending some of my classes on the day of my victorious semifinal match, I took the day of the finals off. As a clear result, I was mentally and physically ready to play, and I defeated the number-two seeded player easily, 6–2, 6–2, for the title.

That night, as I lay in bed, I reflected once again that what appeared to be a devastating loss had actually identified two flaws—my non-focused mind-set and my inadequate pre-match preparation—both of which I needed to change. So I changed them—and secured a cherished victory as a result. This reinforced the fact that a loss on the tennis court or in life, when studied in a non-defensive and honest manner and dealt with constructively, can absolutely be the first step in winning.

The Columbia tournament experiences also taught me that on any given day, in any situation, I can suffer the most heinous loss, but if I choose to remain constructive through the process, I can come back at some point in the future and garner a victory that makes me forget all about the defeat and puts it all in perspective. So even though I lost badly in the Columbia tournament the year before, it was just a loss and a good learning experience. I won the tournament the next year, and even though I had previously embarrassed myself in front of the recruiters, I still wound up being admitted to an excellent college the following year. So I decided that even after the worst losses, I would objectively study the situation, learn what I could, fix the flaw or flaws, and throughout the process, *stay constructive*. I'll have my chance to win again, hopefully sooner rather than later, and I'll redeem myself. And grow to be better in the process.

For someone who absolutely hated to lose, I now view losses very differently. I still don't want or like to lose, but if I'm going to compete, losses are inevitable. My *Strategy* now is: If I have to lose, I will strive to learn as much as I can from the experience, and I'll always remember that a loss today—when studied constructively—can well be the key to coveted wins tomorrow.

Two similar incidents stick out in my mind regarding winning and losing. In March 1995, the UCLA basketball team was playing in the second round of the NCAA Tournament. They were trailing by a point with a little more than four seconds left in the game. Tyus Edney, a UCLA guard, somehow managed to dribble the length of the floor during those few seconds and at the very last instant, lay the ball up to the basket. The ball banked, then finally dropped in just as time ran out. UCLA, as they say, had snatched victory from the jaws of defeat.

If Edney had taken one second more, UCLA would have lost. If the ball had gone an inch to the right or left—no victory. The difference of one second or one inch made winners—and heroes—of UCLA. Had the Bruins lost, Coach Jim Harrick might have been fired; his team had been favored all year to win the national championship. Instead, after UCLA went on to win the tournament and the national title, Harrick was voted coach of the year by the National Association of Basketball Coaches.

On the other hand, the New York Knicks, playing the Houston Rockets in a quarterfinal game of the NBA playoffs a few years ago, trailed by one point with only a few seconds to go. The Knicks' center, Patrick Ewing, had the ball. He drove to the basket and put the ball up with about a half-second left. The ball rolled around the rim—and off. That one inch resulted in a Knick defeat. It may have also resulted in the departure of the team's coach, Pat Riley, who might have felt that his chances of bringing an NBA title to New York would decrease from that point on.

In both of these playoff situations, one inch either way meant triumph or disaster. On another day, the results could have been reversed. Though some will argue that a great champion makes the seconds and inches go his or her way, I want to examine the above scenarios from a *Big-Picture*, non-illusory perspective.

On the ground, day-to-day, our society rewards victories: Wins . . . the big "W." Ultimately, it covets and lauds the end, not the means. Here, I would like to discuss the perspective from the air. I would like to explore the real big "W": Wisdom, and the means along with the ends.

As I discussed earlier, when I used my strengths to pile up victories during my early years, did I really win? Yes and no. Yes, because during my early years, it was very important for me to have the positive reinforcement of being victorious, and to develop the valid feelings of self-esteem, self-worth, and self-love that came with winning. No, because in hindsight, had I allowed myself to suffer more defeats by working harder on my weaker backhand stroke, I undoubtedly would have laid the foundation for many more gratifying victories later.

So depending upon the perspective, what seemed to be wins early on turned out, in reality, to be losses later. Sort of like wine turning to water. Conversely, a client (whom I will discuss later) who was demoted at his TV station initially appeared to have suffered a crushing defeat. But his demotion triggered an escape clause in his station contract, which allowed me to extricate him from it. He was then able to · accept a career-making position in a larger market, at a highly rated and more visible station. Suddenly, the defeat turned into a victory. And water appeared to have turned into champagne.

I would have counseled the team that lost to UCLA on Tyus Edney's layup to fully appreciate the fact that one second or one inch the other way would have meant victory over the eventual national champions. I would have told them to take heart in knowing that they were *this* close to victory, and with just a little improvement in their defense, that they could win the NCAA title the next year. *As a constructive decision-maker, it's important to extract the positives from the perceived negative of the last-second defeat, and build on them.*

Conversely, if I had been working with the UCLA players, I would have told them to take away from the victory the notion, that they were *lucky* or fortunate that day—but for one second or one inch the other way, they would have lost the game. Therefore, they still needed to improve and stay focused, because the difference between winning and losing can be minuscule. If from that point the players could go on to lift their games the following season, their future margins of victory might be bigger.

It is in fact arguable that the UCLA basketball team did not learn enough from its thrilling last-second victory. Throughout the next season, many commentators remarked that some of the UCLA players appeared to be too cocky. Maybe they were. That year, UCLA was upset in the first round of the NCAA playoffs by a team that they would ordinarily beat nine times out of ten. Ironically, they were defeated by a last-second basket!

The key to all of this is how you decide to represent victories and losses to yourself and what positive knowledge and understanding you derive from each. *A mistake or loss remains a mistake or loss only if you don't learn from it.* Objectively dissecting a loss or a setback, and deciding to make a focused effort to learn from your analysis, can be the first step to many wonderful triumphs in the future.

I have found that if you choose to adopt the *Strategy* of perceiving both winning and losing as a means of learning and growing, and not as ends in and of themselves, you will be the true winner in the long run. And in the grand scheme of things, you will attain the real big "W": Wisdom.

Strata-Gems:

- Many of your greatest life lessons can be learned through the experiences of winning and losing.

- Adopting and using the *Strategy* of perceiving both winning and losing as excellent means and opportunities to learn and grow, and not as ends in and of themselves, can help you to become a wiser and more enhancing decision-maker and a much more successful and self-fulfilled individual.

- In order to develop strong and valid feelings of self-worth, identify things that you've done well, in addition to taking a constructive approach, when correcting and/or eliminating your missteps.

- A mistake or loss remains a mistake or loss *only* if you don't learn from it.

SPONTANEITY

There are times in life to be disciplined and structured, and to delay gratification. There are other occasions, however, when all discipline, structure, and guilt should be thrown out, and we should be . . . spontaneous. That is, we should go with what *feels right at the moment*.

"Appropriateness" is the determining factor as to whether spontaneity should govern your decision. Essentially, you must decide, after you've weighed your true values, whether being spontaneous is appropriate in the situation at hand, and whether or not it allows you to attain your most cherished values.

Two quick stories. It was a Sunday in March, and I had just become a news agent at the William Morris Agency. A week or so earlier, I had been given a tip that there were two female anchors, both living and anchoring in the same small Southern city, who were going to become superstars. During the preceding few days, I had received videotapes of their work. The tip was in fact correct. They were definitely great talents in the making. However, until that day, I hadn't been able to reach either one of them on the phone.

When I finally spoke to one, she explained that she was interested in discussing representation with me, but that "our timing might not be right." She explained that she was about to fly to a job interview on Monday afternoon and would have to make a decision immediately thereafter upon her return home Tuesday night. And she didn't want to be represented by anyone whom she hadn't met and talked with face to face. So, she reasoned, it might be better if we put off representation discussions for a year or so, until she'd settled in her new job and had time to meet me in person.

As she finished expressing her thoughts, I quickly decided that I couldn't wait much longer to secure her representation, because once other top agents heard about her and saw her work, she'd be deluged with representation offers, and the percentages of my signing her would materially decrease.

I realized that I had to do something now. Why not something spontaneous? "I'm going to drive to the nearest airport, catch a plane, and we'll either meet later tonight or first thing tomorrow morning," I told her. Surprised and flattered that I'd consider doing something so dramatic, she responded, "God, that would be wonderful, but are you sure you want to go to all that trouble? We can wait a while." Without giving her time to change her mind, I quickly responded, "I'll call you from the airport in about an hour and I'll let you know when I'll be arriving."

"I'm excited," she said.

"Me, too. I look forward to talking with you, soon," I replied. Then I raced to the airport.

About 11:45 that evening, after her newscast, we met for about an hour or so. The next morning, she called me at my hotel and told me the good news: We would be a team.

An hour later, I met the other talented anchor for breakfast. She, too, signed with me. Because both of these women, with my help, made very big and visible career jumps, I was then able to sign many other talented individuals at a very pivotal point in my young representation career. This materially enhanced my stature in the business. Clearly, being spontaneous worked incredibly well for me in this instance.

Come to think of it, I employed the *Strategy* of spontaneity in becoming Matt Lauer's agent, as well. When I called Matt for the first time, I quickly realized that his career was at a pivotal and problematic juncture, because he was just about to leave his position as a host of a morning show on WWOR in New York. Because of the timing in

Matt's career and the magnitude of what I perceived his potential to be, I told him that I would fly to New York from L.A. that afternoon and we would meet for lunch the following day.

During lunch, we discussed Matt's career, his aspirations, and my perceptions and recommendations. I remember being taken by the fact that Matt was as warm, real, and quick-witted in person as he was on the air. We bonded, and I was fortunate enough to become his agent. Matt eventually joined WNBC in New York, and then the *Today* show. To this day, I'm appreciative to be Matt's agent, and thrilled to be his good friend.

All of these very positive things took place because at *Crunch Time*, I decided to employ the enhancing and constructive *Strategy* of being spontaneous.

Strata-Gem:

There are times in life to be disciplined and to delay gratification, and there are other instances that call for you to be spontaneous and go for it, then and there. The key is to decide what is the appropriate strategy to implement, given the specific situation or issue that you're faced with.

BEING CONSTRUCTIVE, ADAPTABLE, AND FLEXIBLE: HITTING THE BALL WHERE IT'S PITCHED

I learned at an early age how important the *Strategies* of being flexible and adaptable are to making constructive and emotionally intelligent decisions. In my junior year of college, I was chosen to be a member of the United States tennis team that would travel to Israel to compete in the Maccabiah Games. This was great news. But there was bad news, too. Two weeks before my departure, while training in Miami Beach, I began to run a high fever. My energy was gone. It became hard to swallow, and I lost my appetite—even for ice cream and other desserts. An absolute first!

I went to see a neighborhood doctor in Miami Beach. Big mistake. While in the waiting room, I noticed that everyone there looked *really* old. Upon meeting the doctor, he took one look at me and blurted out, "You're the healthiest specimen I've seen in years." Of course, he hadn't seen anyone under eighty in years, either.

He did a cursory examination, and with great confidence rendered his opinion. He said that I had flu-like symptoms and that my glands were swollen, but that if I took some antibiotics, I'd be up and around in a couple of days.

I did. And I wasn't.

Five days later, I returned to school with the same symptoms, and I was losing weight quickly. I went to the infirmary and the doctor immediately had me take a blood test. The next day, I learned that I had a severe case of mononucleosis, which was weird, because I had been diagnosed with mono when I was seven years old, and I had always been told that you couldn't contract mono twice.

The doctor told me that my glands and spleen were quite swollen. There could be no debate. Not only could I not play tennis for a few months, I couldn't fly with the team to Israel, either. I would be bedridden.

I was completely blown away. I had really been looking forward to taking my first trip abroad and playing in Israel. I went back to my room, calmed down, and reminded myself that things do happen for a reason. The key is to be constructive and make the most of what was presented to me. It didn't take much for me to figure out what being constructive called for in this instance.

My grades that year were critical. They would determine where I would be accepted to graduate school. During the Christmas break, which I had used to go to Miami and prepare for the Maccabiah Games, and in the three weeks after that, when I was scheduled to travel to and compete in Israel, I should have been studying for my upcoming exams.

In my *Heart-of-Hearts*, I knew that with all of my Maccabiah-related activities, there was no way that I would be able to adequately prepare for my exams. Getting mononucleosis gave me the opportunity to do just that.

So disappointed, but determined to make the most of my time in bed, I studied long and hard. I even came up with an intriguing and original concept for my senior thesis, which I titled "How to Select a Jury to the Advantage of a Client." It would be based upon decision-making theories that our class had studied, along with empirical research that I would do. I thought my advisor would flip over the idea, and he did. My grades rose substantially that semester. My honors thesis was deemed "groundbreaking," and I ended up graduating magna cum laude. This enabled me to be accepted into some of the most attractive grad-school programs. Due to my thesis topic, I also learned a bit about our legal system, and this exposure prompted me to go to law school.

I never again had the opportunity to play in the Maccabiah Games.

But after I received my grades and was well on my way to completing my thesis, I realized that I was happy with the self-enhancing way in which I had decided to handle the whole situation.

Great hitters in baseball often say that they've learned to "hit the ball where it's pitched." They get up to the plate and remain open and flexible. Instead of waiting for one pitch—usually their favorite pitch, which may or may not ever come. They take whatever pitch is thrown to them and adapt their swing in an appropriate and effective manner. They meet the pitch with firmness and confidence, yet with an adaptable, "soft-hands" approach. More often than most, they get a hit.

These hitters are constructive decision-makers.

Great hitters in life have the same approach. I've seen this from my dad on many occasions. These individuals are courageously ready to deal with whatever life serves up to them: good or bad, unexpected or not. They know that stuff happens—that's life—but unlike others, they don't back out or duck away from the tough or uncomfortable pitches of life. They choose to make a conscious effort to stay strong at the plate and deal flexibly and firmly with whatever life throws at them.

Great hitters in baseball often relish the challenge of facing tough odds and thriving. And while great hitters in life don't always savor facing life's problems and the often painful growth attached to this process, they do know that constructively facing life's problems is a necessary discipline for living life in a vital and passionate way. Their perspective? *It's something ya gotta do, so do it constructively.*

Being constructive, by meeting and hitting the ball where it's pitched, can often pay huge dividends.

A conversation that I had a few years ago with a news executive who has done more than anyone to revolutionize local news over the past decade aptly illustrates the concepts of being constructive and flexible when presented with various stimuli.

When I asked him why he thought that he and his stations had become so successful, he enthusiastically replied: "It's because my station managers have complete flexibility. Other stations have hard, etched-in-stone rules and ways of doing things that take months to change. They also have talent contracts that guarantee that their on-camera people must anchor and report for specific shows. We, on the other hand, have designed our operations so that we can change things within a couple of hours. We can creatively and flexibly respond to the always-changing environment. We can change our tone, our focus, and even vary which shows our talent anchors and reports on. This allows us to be both more responsive to the news of the day and to the needs and desires of our viewers. Basically, when a news opportunity presents itself, unlike other stations, we can jump on it and make it our own."

This very successful news executive knows: If you can respond to the stimuli that come your way flexibly, sensitively, and with "soft hands" and positively and responsively create and seize opportunities, these *Strategies* can pay great decision-making dividends.

Strata-Gem:

The decision to deal with events, challenges, and problems in a flexible manner can be very constructive and self-enhancing. People who are successful and achieve their goals are often adaptable in dealing with whatever comes their way.

THINGS HAPPEN FOR A REASON

In life, things sometimes work out as planned. Sometimes they don't. The issues are: How do you choose to perceive and value the events in your life and those that take place in the lives of others? And do you decide to actively seize upon them and make the most of them?

About ninety years ago, my grandfather, who was then fighting in the Polish Army, contracted some sort of blood poisoning and died quickly thereafter. He was thirty-two years old. Because of this devastating turn of events, my dad, his mother, and his baby sister quickly accepted their relatives' long-standing offer to leave Poland, come to the United States, and move in with them in their Brooklyn apartment. This was an offer that they never would have accepted if my grandfather had still been alive and fighting in Poland. Ten days after my grandfather's death, my father and his family left their hometown of Krakow and began their trip to the U.S. That afternoon, just hours after they left, enemy soldiers invaded Krakow and captured many of its inhabitants—including all of our relatives, who were all killed.

My father believes that his father died so that my father, his sister, and his mother could live. And while this may be an effective rationalization to explain and cope with a profoundly sad event, the facts are clear: Were it not for my grandfather's untimely death, my father and his family, in all likelihood, would have been captured and killed along with all of the other inhabitants of his town.

I believe that there are few individuals like my father, who passionately love life and savor every moment here on earth. My father has often recounted stories of all of the fighting and bloodshed that engulfed him and those who lived in his Polish town, and how fortunate he was to survive. The insights that I have gleaned from this portion of my dad's life are many.

I learned that when you walk with the shadow of death hanging over your shoulder, you can truly appreciate every moment of life and relish it. While living in Poland, the specter of death was always looming. Having his young father pass away in a relative instant certainly made my father more aware of how fragile and fleeting life can be. I believe that my dad developed his passion for life because of his traumatic childhood experiences and uncertain environment.

I have also come to learn to expect the good, the bad, and the devastating in life. They are part of the life process. In watching and listening to my father, I have learned to value the act and courage of dealing with the triumphs and disasters of life in an active and constructive manner, and to endeavor to make every experience an opportunity to learn, to become wiser, and to nourish my soul and spirit.

My dad learned some invaluable lessons from the death of his father. My dad's constructive attitude didn't bring his father back to life on earth, or make the pain of death any less severe. It did, however, teach him to live a more active, appreciative, and enthusiastic life.

I also learned, and now sincerely believe, that things often happen for a reason. We may view these things or events in our lives as initially "positive" or "negative." However, time often proves that they are not at all as we first perceived. The one thing that I do know is that everything that happens to us, and around us, is a life-lesson from which to learn. It is written in the popular book *The Celestine Prophecy*, that "there are no coincidences." I believe this. Make it your mission, as a constructive decision-maker, to learn as much as you can from those around you, and from what happens to you and to others. Here are a few stories about deciding to constructively deal with the pitches we're thrown.

After completing law school, I was about to be offered a position that I coveted at an entertainment sports law firm when an individual at that firm was served with divorce papers and chose not to leave as planned. His change of plans resulted in the firm deciding at the eleventh hour not to offer me the only law firm position that I would have accepted at that time. I was very disappointed.

A few weeks later, I interviewed with a Miami law firm. During the interview, the senior partner and others focused on my academic background. However, I concentrated on the tennis business that I had developed, and how I, at the age of twenty-one, and the many tennis pros who were teaching with me were instructing hundreds of people each week. I twice raised the point that just as I did all of the marketing and client recruitment for that business, I could also bring in clients to their firm. I loved people, and people seemed to trust me.

Two days later, I learned that I didn't get the job. I was told by the senior partner that I had placed so much emphasis on being personally involved in bringing clients to the firm that the partners were afraid that I wouldn't be focused enough on doing the vast amounts of research and writing that the position demanded. He also said that apparently they didn't need more clients. The partner finished by telling me that he agreed that I'd be great with people, and that whatever jobs that I might consider taking should incorporate that ability.

Okay. So once again, I was back to square one and not feeling great. But I knew that I needed to stay constructive and proactive until the right opportunity could be created. About a month later, I interviewed with an entertainment law firm that seemed interesting. In researching the firm, I learned that it was the outside counsel to the William Morris Agency. I told my dad about this, because his best childhood friend was the current president of the agency. My dad suggested that I fly to Los Angeles and visit with his friend. Maybe he could write a recommendation to the law firm for me. I did just that.

A week later, I met the president of William Morris for what turned out to be a two-hour dinner and an hour-and-a-half walk through Beverly Hills. My dad's friend loved my athletic background and the way in which had I built my business. Most of all, he appreciated my love of people. Throughout our meeting, he passionately talked about the agenting, or "people," business. At the time, William Morris represented, or had in the past represented, such individuals as Elvis Presley, Barbara Walters, James Michener, The Beatles, Robert Redford, Goldie Hawn, and others.

When dinner was over, he said that he was *not* going to recommend me to his law firm, but instead, wanted me to come work at William Morris. He said, "I'm going to personally design a path for you. We'll start you out as an attorney and teach you everything we can while you work in business affairs. Then we'll make you an agent. You'll be a *great* agent." I replied, "Mr. Weisbord, please don't take this the wrong way, but an agent sounds like some greasy, sleazy guy with a ring on his pinkie, three gold chains around his neck, and a shirt unbuttoned down to his navel, who says, 'I'm gonna make you a star, baby!' That's just not me." He countered with, "There are sleazy doctors, sleazy lawyers, and sleazy politicians. We choose to do our business honorably. If we didn't, we wouldn't represent the caliber of people that we do."

He made sense. My heart sang! I knew that I had found my *Heart-of-Hearts* career: working with and developing talented and interesting people.

Our meeting took place almost twenty-four years ago. Today, I still love what I do. The constructive decision in this instance was my staying proactive regarding my job search and choosing to fly to Los Angeles to meet Mr. Weisbord, even though I never expected that I would wind up working for his company.

Years ago, I received a call from a news manager regarding an extraordinarily talented newscaster client of mine. The manager told me that despite my client's obvious talent, he didn't "fit in" with the station's format and presentation and would be demoted in about two weeks to a lesser anchor role. I immediately called my client to give him the disheartening news, knowing how devastated he would be.

After his initial shock and trauma wore off, sadness (about having to pick up and move yet again), anger, and fear started to set in. During the process, I assured my client and his family that *things happen for a reason*.

Sometimes we don't always immediately see why, but they do; and that perceived negatives can be true learning experiences and *opportunities to seize other valuable experiences*. I told him and his family that the good news in all of this was that when a very talented person that I represent suffers a setback, or cannot for some reason accept what appears to be a great opportunity, something better or more appropriate almost always comes along later. I continued by telling my client and his family that I had to be intelligently and creatively proactive in making that better or more appropriate opportunity come along as quickly as possible. I also counseled my client to remain positive and constructive by being as good as he could be on his lower-profile newscast, even though he was feeling psychologically and emotionally down and disappointed. Amazingly and serendipitously, a few days after our talk an executive from a top-market station happened to be in town, and he saw my client anchoring. He thought that my client was great, and three weeks later he hired him for a major anchor job. In retrospect, my client's devastating experience turned out to be the best thing that could have happened. It allowed me to market him and then extricate him from his contract.

My client later called and thanked me for believing in him and counseling him through it all. I commended him for remaining constructive during the dark and uncertain times, because if he had decided to let his unhappiness show on the air, the executive passing through town would never have hired him. My client had indeed made the very most of an initially negative situation.

Another client, Dayna Devon, was working in Memphis as the anchor of all of her station's weeknight newscasts. From the time I started representing Dayna, she always dreamed of hosting a national entertainment news show such as *EXTRA*, *Entertainment Tonight*, or *Access Hollywood*.

One day, I received a call from a news executive of a Houston, Texas, station, who wanted to fly Dayna in for an interview and audition. Dayna was excited about the opportunity because she was eager to grow and at the same time be geographically closer to her family. However, I was less enthusiastic about it. I didn't see it as the right next career step; I felt that she could eventually do better.

The audition and interview at the station didn't go well. Dayna, being relatively young, had little or no experience in the auditioning process, and as a result, she came off as a bit green and inexperienced. By the time she was finished with all of her meetings and was on her way to the airport, I had already spoken to the news manager of the station that auditioned her. That manager told me that Dayna had great potential, but that she wasn't quite ready for the job. She needed to be a bit "more seasoned" and "well-prepared."

When Dayna arrived at the airport, she called me to tell me how poorly the meetings and audition had gone. She explained the station managers had asked her in-depth questions about the station and its parent company, and she was at a loss, as neither she nor I thought that these subjects would be the basis of interview questions.

When I told her that she wasn't going to get the job, she was devastated. I felt bad for her, but I believed and counseled her that things happen for a reason, and that she wasn't supposed to get *that* job. However, she *was* supposed to learn from the experience, so when the *right* position for her did become available, she'd nail both the audition and the interview. "Just learn from this and stay constructive," I advised her.

A couple of days later, when the sting of the disappointment began to dissipate, Dayna called me and said, "OK, let's go over what I did wrong, so that it never happens again." A very constructive decision, and we did exactly that.

About six months later, a weekend anchor job on *EXTRA* became available. Despite the concerns of the show's executive producer that my client was too young and too inexperienced for the job, he trusted my recommendation and flew Dayna in for an interview and audition. She arrived in Los Angeles the day before the interview, so that she'd be well rested and relaxed for the next day's meetings. (Another constructive decision.) We had dinner that night, and I was blown away by how well-prepared she was. She knew everything about the history of the show, its executive producer, and the company that produced it. She had taped ten days' worth of shows and had carefully studied the anchor's delivery and body language, as well as *EXTRA*'s content.

Dayna's interviews and audition went smashingly. After about three months of waiting, she was offered the weekend anchor position. When I told Dayna the good news, she cried with happiness. I was thrilled beyond belief for her, because she is a wonderful person who had taken a defeat and made it a constructive learning experience.

After we calmed down, I reinforced my perspective by telling her, "See, things happen for a reason. You weren't supposed to get that other job. You were meant to have that experience *and learn from it* . . . and you did. I'm thrilled for you, but even more importantly, I respect and admire you."

Approximately three and a half years later, Dayna was promoted to her ultimate dream position—the main host of *EXTRA*.

Sometimes you're lucky—you quickly gain an insight as to why something happened, *and* the direct result of the occurrence is positive. This was the case for Dayna Devon, who secured her dream hosting job after being turned down for a job in the local market. Sometimes, however, you may only eventually learn of the ultimate impact of certain occurrences. You might learn this in the context of some other event that occurs years later that you also learn from. You must also remember that the events of life's learning process, in retrospect, won't always be positive. For my male anchor client, they were positive. He was demoted; this afforded me the opportunity to find for him and for him to accept a great new job. Everything worked out fine. However, for my father, there was nothing positive about a young boy suddenly losing a young father whom he deeply loved. Events don't always work out for the best. *But you can choose to take the best things from these events and make the most of them.*

The first sentence of M. Scott Peck's *A Road Less Traveled*, is "Life is difficult." It often is. But from these difficulties come lessons and wonderful opportunities from which you can learn and grow. The key is how you perceive these opportunities and whether you positively and constructively seize them. When you choose to learn from the lessons before you, however difficult or disappointing they may be, you become wiser and better equipped to face similar and/or new situations as you continue to travel down the road of life. And as we've discussed, what might be a disappointment now could turn out to be the foundation for a triumph later.

As I step back and look at the *Big Picture*, I clearly see that things often do happen for a reason. In my dad's case, if his father hadn't suddenly died, he and his family in all likelihood would have stayed and been killed in Poland. If I had gotten and accepted the law firm position in Miami, I wouldn't have interviewed with the entertainment law firm, which ultimately led me to work for the William Morris Agency. If I had gone to Israel and played in the Maccabiah Games, as I discussed in the previous chapter, I wouldn't have received the grades that I did during my all-important junior year in college. If Dayna Devon had gotten the anchor job in the top market, she never would have been contractually available to audition for and accept her dream position as the host of *EXTRA*, etc.

As we've discussed, an important lesson that I have learned through athletics is that I can suffer a stinging defeat today, but if I stay proactive and constructive, I can have a resounding victory tomorrow, next week, or next year that puts the loss in perspective and relieves the sting. From this, I have decided that no matter what the setback, and no matter how disappointing or devastating it is, I will choose to constructively go on and make the best of it. I will choose not to retreat, go into a funk, or become negative, for at least four reasons:

1) As we discussed earlier, the concepts of winning and losing can be illusions.
2) In my *Heart-of-Hearts*, I believe that things do happen for a reason, and that if I stay poised and I proactively seize the opportunities that are presented—or if I proactively create them—things will come together and I will learn an important lesson.

3) Few positive things can occur when one is feeling sorry for oneself, in a funk, depressed, or withdrawn.

4) I have seen people who are negative and who let their defeats consume them. They often become bitter, sarcastic, and/or defeated. These responses are neither physically nor emotionally healthy or productive.

Strata-Gem:

It is quite possible that many things in life happen for a reason. Whether you believe this or not, one thing is clear: How you decide to perceive and deal with the events in your life and those that occur in the lives of relevant others will determine how constructive, happy, and fulfilled your life is.

THE IMPORTANCE OF EFFECTIVE
COMMUNICATION

During my many years as a career counselor, I've always been amazed at how many times a ruptured relationship is caused by poor communication. Trust me, more important relationships go sour due to this problem than you can imagine. As a result, I find myself sharing with my clients the following two related *Strategies* many times each day:

1) Make sure to initiate and/or maintain good and accurate communication between yourself and relevant others; and
2) Make the effort to listen and truly hear what others are telling you.

In connection with good communication, a story about an anchor client of mine, "Gina," and her older, more established male coanchor, "Ed," comes to mind. Gina is one of the nicest, most giving people I know. Her problem was that Ed treated her poorly. He often wouldn't talk to her while they were on the set, and he was often dismissive and condescending to her when they did speak. This very unpleasant state of affairs was eating away at Gina. As a result, she was contemplating either going to management and getting Ed removed from their very prestigious newscast, or quitting her high-profile and otherwise very rewarding job.

I counseled Gina that neither alternative was a constructive or appropriate strategy to pursue without first attempting to sit down—out of the office—with Ed and establishing a truce and an effective line of communication. I suggested to Gina that she be the bigger person and invite Ed out to lunch. I'd even pay for it. She took my advice, and after some procrastination on Ed's part, they dined.

As they spoke, Gina learned that Ed's negative behavior could be traced to his perception that the relatively young and very attractive Gina had gotten her position without "paying her dues." That in essence, she was hired and quickly elevated to be his coanchor because of her good looks. However, when Ed learned that Gina had put herself through college and journalism grad school by working as a newswriter and producer, and that she had an extensive overseas reporting background, his demeanor noticeably changed.

By the end of the lunch, not only had mutual respect been established, but they also learned that they shared similar journalistic philosophies.

A week or so later, Gina and Ed and their respective spouses enjoyed a three-hour dinner. Since that time, they've been the closest of friends, and their on-air chemistry has gone from problematic to excellent.

All of these good things transpired because of Gina's constructive decision to establish good communication with Ed.

Another story illustrates the importance of initiating both effective and "touching" communication.

My mom always had a hypoactive thyroid, which resulted in her moving very slowly and lethargically. Not surprisingly, she was often late for appointments, but her tardiness was only partially due to her physical condition. The other part, she knows, was the result of her own environmental adaptation. Throughout my mom's childhood, she was criticized by her mother for being "slow," "stupid," and "good for nothing." My mom remembers being about four years old when she realized that her mother was poisonous and decided to be nothing like her. She began to search for a different female role model. Years later, my mom chose one: an attractive, statuesque film star named Kay Francis, who was always portrayed as a picture-perfect, elegant model. Ms. Francis was the exact opposite of my mom's mother, whom she perceived as slovenly and sloppy.

Thereafter, my mom always had to look picture-perfect in order to emulate Ms. Francis. It took her hours to get ready for any appointment or occasion, major or minor. As my mom tells it, she wouldn't take the trash out without being fully dressed and made up, like a model ready for a runway appearance. The result of her extensive preparation was that she was always late. She was late for school and for work. She was late for every important date. She was late for interviews. She was late for her best friend's wedding. She was late for her sister's wedding. She was late for her own wedding.

Her mother consistently berated and often beat her for dawdling and being late. Countless others who were affected by her lateness routinely criticized her. All to no avail. Nothing anybody said or did seemed to make any impression on her.

Then, one fateful, frigid winter day, my mom kept my dad waiting on a street corner for more than two hours. As my mom tells it, when she finally arrived at their appointed meeting place outside the theater, my dad was nearly apoplectic. He looked like he was ready to foam at the mouth. It was clear that he was fighting hard to control his massive anger. My mom apologized profusely and sincerely, over and over again. He didn't say a word. His rage seemed to be overwhelming. My mom grew apprehensive. She didn't know what was going to happen. Without saying a word, my dad checked his watch, turned his back on my mom, and walked rapidly into the theater. They had planned to have dinner before going to the show. My mom was now worried that my dad would be hungry—and she was hungry, too. But under the circumstances, she meekly followed my dad into the theater. They sat in silence. At the intermission, my dad rose from his seat and announced in a hoarse whisper that he was leaving. My mom got up and followed him out of the theater and into the garage where the car was parked. They drove home in total, deadly silence.

The next day, Saturday, my dad still wasn't speaking. He left the house very early; my mom had a sleepless night.

At about 2:00 P.M. on Sunday, my mom was in her dressing room in front of the mirror, putting on her makeup à la Kay Francis. Quietly, my dad came into the room. He observed my mom silently. She saw his reflection in the mirror, but remained silent, waiting for him to speak.

"Betty," he began, in a very tight, controlled voice, "I don't know what to say. I don't exactly know how to tell you this, but I simply don't understand you. Your behavior is an absolute mystery to me. If you were stupid, *then* I could understand, and I might forgive you. But you're one of the most intelligent people I know. And, generally, I think you're a very nice person. So I ask you this: How can you be so completely thoughtless? So inconsiderate? How can you be so downright *mean*?! To *me*? How could you let me wait on a street corner for two whole hours on such a freezing cold night? It's beyond me. I can't begin to tell you how hurt I am. I wouldn't do to a dog what you did to me. How can you be so uncaring, so impossibly *mean*? How could you? It doesn't make any sense at all. I just don't know anymore. That's it—I'm done."

My dad turned on his heel and walked out. My mom was stunned. She instantly stopped applying her mascara. She had never before thought of herself as being particularly thoughtless or inconsiderate. She definitely never thought that she was in any conceivable way *mean*. *Mean* was the key word, the *trigger*. It bothered her greatly, striking a primal chord somewhere deep in her psyche. She was aware that she was feeling extremely defensive. My mom was psychologically savvy enough to know that her strong defensiveness was a clear signal—a warning. Attention needed to be paid. She understood that something of great importance for her had just happened. At that moment, she allowed herself to be open and honest enough to accept that the things my dad had just told her were valid in some profoundly meaningful way that she didn't yet fully comprehend.

My mom says she knew in her gut that it was absolutely imperative that she take the time to make a concerted effort to analyze her behavior, her feelings, and her visceral responses as they related to the words, thoughts, and feelings that my dad had shared with her.

My mom didn't move from the spot in front of the mirror. She just sat there and thought long and hard. Years later, this is what she told me about it.

To begin with, my mom checked her feelings. She knew that she was sincerely sorry she'd hurt my dad. She also definitely knew that she wasn't being intentionally *mean*. She really and truly cared for my dad.

My mom recalled that after each and every one of her negative experiences related to her lateness, she felt wholly unable to rectify her behavior to any appreciable degree. Up to that point in time, she was still terribly frustrated, still feeling helpless, and, according to her, hopeless in the face of this persistent problem. In fact, my mom was so traumatized by her constant failure in this area of her life that she was very uncomfortable even thinking about it. She usually kidded around and made light about it on the outside (e.g., "But I'm so great when I finally *do* get there"). Inwardly, however, she was extremely upset with herself. She was angry at her impotence and ashamed at her inability to overcome this generally trivial but apparently insurmountable problem for her. After so many years, she still couldn't figure out the source of the problem. She knew better intellectually, but for some reason she couldn't "do better" in reality. This was the sad case, despite all the trouble and heartache that she and those she loved had to endure as a result of her persistent lateness.

My mother wondered why she was so very disturbed when my dad said she was mean. Then it hit her. Her mother was mean—the *Queen of Mean*—and in no way would my mom want to be like her. That was *it!* That's why she was so disturbed by being called mean. She was being like her mother, a person for whom she had very little respect. This was profoundly appalling to her.

This distasteful recognition slowly sank in—deeply. My mom looked at herself in the mirror and could hardly believe what she was thinking and what she was finally beginning to comprehend and see clearly. For all practical intents and purposes, she had been stone-cold blind to the facts that being late meant being mean and incredibly inconsiderate, and that she had been late every day of her life.

She then came to another truly shocking realization. Chills shot through her body. It was because she so abhorred her mother that my mom chose to be just like her father . . . *and her father was always late!*

A few moments later, my mom decided to figure out a *Strategy* right then and there so that she wouldn't repeat her past mistakes. She knew she would have to start with a few achievable baby steps so there would be no chance of failing again.

She began by setting her watch ahead by two hours, so that she would get a much earlier start. From that day on, my mom changed her hairstyle so that it required much less maintenance. And she rarely, if ever, wears her makeup as she used to. This saves her loads of time. Gradually, she was able to set all of her clocks ahead by one and a half hours; then one hour; then by half an hour; then by fifteen minutes. Eventually, her watch and clocks were set to the real time. Now my mom often arrives early for appointments. My dad and I are both amazed.

These changes are a reflection of my mom's keen awareness of her past destructive behavior. They also more accurately represent my mom's true value system, which places a higher value on being thoughtful and considerate of others than on receiving compliments for looking perfect.

As a direct result of my dad's honest insight into my mom's mean behavior, he was able to effectively communicate with and *touch* my mom as no one ever had. Because my dad understood my mom and *how* to *touch* her, he was able to get her to shatter her seemingly etched-in-stone status quo.

Along with being an effective communicator, there is no more enhancing ability to develop and wise *Strategy* to adopt and implement than being or becoming an active and skilled listener. By doing this, you can grow to understand where the communicator is coming from and what he or she is really saying and trying to accomplish through their communications.

For example, in connection with the Miami law firm interview that I discussed in the preceding chapter, had I been a better listener to the person who interviewed me, I would have picked up on the fact that he wanted to hear more about my interest in performing day-to-day legal work and much less about my passion for bringing in new clients. In hindsight, I'm happy that I wasn't offered that job, but I learned a valuable lesson: I need to be a skilled and intuitive listener *if I'm going to truly connect with others.*

When I was a young agent and had a million things going on at the same time, two of my clients told me that they felt that I wasn't truly listening to them. One of these clients said that she felt that I might not be the "right" representative for her because of this deficiency. Fortunately, I took the concerns of those two clients seriously. I realized that as good as I was at finding ability-appropriate jobs for my clients, being a good listener and counselor, according to some clients' value systems, was even more important to them than my job-searching abilities. From that day on, I became a better listener, and as a direct result, a much more effective advisor and teammate, because in order to be a good advisor, I must be a good listener.

In another relevant story, there was a very quick-witted host that I represented years ago named Chris. Chris's career got off to a relatively slow start, but he quickly received a great deal of positive attention when he became the anchor of an entertainment news show. His razor-sharp, sarcastic wit was what made him stand out as he delivered the entertainment news of the day. Then, a couple of years later, he was given the coveted job of hosting a major network interview program. The problem was that Chris was so used to playing everything for the laugh as the anchor of his entertainment news show that he just assumed that this same strategy would work for his interviews. It didn't. When his guests would attempt to answer one of his questions, Chris would often interrupt them and interject a joke or a sarcastic remark—before the guest finished answering. In essence, Chris was so focused on making the moment his instead of his guests' that he was perceived by many to be a very selfish and self-indulgent non-listener. Obviously, neither quality is attractive or endearing on-air—or in real life.

Besides sticking to his always-go-for-the-joke strategy, which worked for him as an anchor but was totally inappropriate in the role of an interviewer, I also believe that choosing not to listen to his guests' answers was in many ways a defense mechanism for Chris. By always making quick jokes, Chris avoided having any real, deep intimacy or connection with his guests. I see this destructive defensive strategy adopted and acted out by individuals in real life situations all the time and it is often *toxic* to relationships.

It wasn't until a couple of months after Chris had become the host of the interview show—and "A-List" guests and audience viewership began to dwindle at a precipitous rate—that Chris finally got the message: If you want to connect with someone, show them that you respect them and that you truly desire to hear what it is that they are telling you. The key is to be an open, objective, and active listener. Once again, you can accomplish this by giving the person with whom you are speaking respect and attention. This is a constructive *Strategy* for everyone to adopt, not just network interviewers.

Strata-Gem:

- One of the most constructive *Strategies* that you can adopt is to make sure that you have good, effective, and accurate communication with others.
- If you want to be an effective and wise decision-maker, be an active, objective, intuitive, and respectful listener.

ONE CHARACTER MISSTEP CAN NULLIFY
ALL OF THE GREAT THINGS YOU'VE DONE

As I was editing and polishing this book, four news stories caught my attention.

1) Kobe Bryant was charged with criminal sexual assault. If convicted of the charge, he could face four years to life in prison. As a result of this situation, his squeaky clean image has been ruined. (Note: Criminal charges have since been dropped.)

2) A federal grand jury indicted Martha Stewart on charges of conspiracy, obstruction of justice, and making false statements to investigators. (Note: Stewart has since been found guilty of four counts of securities fraud.)

3) *Living History*, a new book by Hillary Rodham Clinton, was released. The book, in part, discusses former President Clinton's affair with Monica Lewinsky and the impact that it had on his marriage, presidency, and legacy.

4) Sammy Sosa, one of Major League Baseball's most prolific all-time home run hitters and one of its most popular and marketable personalities, was found to have used an illegally corked bat in a regular-season game. This statement from *Today* show reporter Kevin Tibbles says it all: "Sosa's record

Today show, June 5, 2003.

will be tarnished forever."* A *Los Angeles Times* headline from June 5, 2003, reads "Besides Bat, Sosa's Image May Have Been Shattered."* This is a sad story about someone who was a hero to many. Sad, because one mistake—made knowingly or otherwise—has negatively impacted his life and legacy forever.

As a constructive decision-maker, the thing to glean from the Kobe Bryant, Martha Stewart, Bill Clinton, and (possibly) Sammy Sosa stories is that when reaching their final decisions, it appears as if all of them, for one reason or another, completely ignored the potential gravity of doing something they knew to be wrong. It also appears as if they didn't seriously, realistically, or fully consider the potential damage to themselves, to their careers, to those they love and those who love them, and to many others around them. In addition, it appears as if they totally ignored the possibility that they could get caught. The fact is, they did get caught, and the damage they caused to all concerned may be irreparable.

In studying the stories of all four of these individuals, as well as similar ones from the past, I've observed that one really bad decision—especially if it involves a display of poor character, or the complete lack of character—can tarnish *all* of the very good things you may have previously accomplished. Unfortunately, it is also quite possible that even an unintentional mistake can override all of the good that you've done up to that point. For example, take Sammy Sosa's situation. Sosa claims that he used his corked batting-practice bat in a real game, but that he honestly didn't know it. It was a mistake. His explanation, in some ways, is supported by the fact that his other seventy-six bats in the Chicago Cubs clubhouse were found to have no trace of cork. So even if Sosa is telling the truth, he has nonetheless been publicly humiliated, and in many ways vilified. Additionally, he will have to live with the lingering cloud and speculation that no one will ever truly know how many, if any, of his 500-plus home runs were hit with an illegal bat.

*Page A30.

Another point regarding self-enhancing decision-making is relevant here. When I was in seventh grade, one of my classes was devoted to "Ethics." I've always remembered my ethics teacher telling us, "Never bend down to tie your shoe in a watermelon patch. Why? Because, it will appear as if you are bending over to steal a watermelon, and this appearance—even if it has no basis in fact—can lead people to think that you are a thief. So always remember: Be careful not to do the wrong thing—or even appear to do the wrong thing—because both can have negative consequences."

During law school, I studied the *Legal Code of Ethics*. Embodied in that code was the same real-life *Strategy* that my elementary school ethics teacher sought to instill in us: "[Attorneys] should avoid even the appearance of impropriety." This is great decision-making advice for attorneys and non-attorneys alike. For example, Kobe Bryant, who is married, allowed or invited the alleged assault victim into his hotel room. Even if Kobe is innocent of the alleged sexual assault charge, constructive and self-enhancing decision-making dictates—in fact, absolutely demands!—that he not have a woman in his hotel room, because it appears improper, and this apparent impropriety *alone* could put his career, his image, and his personal life in jeopardy.

Besides the appearance of impropriety issue, just having a woman in your room late at night (or at any other time) is a potentially self-sabotaging decision for any married man, because you significantly increase the chances that something very damaging will happen. In Kobe's case, it certainly did.

I am a strong advocate of the *Strategy* that just because you *can* do something wrong, questionable, or inappropriate and maybe get away with it, doesn't mean that you *should* do it. Or, put another way, just because you believe that you have the power, anonymity, access, or perceived protection to get away with something that you know is wrong, doesn't mean that you should engage in that activity. It also doesn't mean that you'll continue to get away with it. This is a wholly self-sabotaging attitude and belief.

President Clinton certainly had the opportunity to have affairs with many women, and perhaps he thought that because of his power and position he could get away with them by hiding them or lying about them (even during a nationally televised address), so he decided to indulge himself. Maybe the executives at Enron, because of their seemingly secure positions, thought that they could bilk the public and suffer no consequences. Maybe Martha Stewart thought that she could perform illegal acts and get away with them. Similarly, maybe Kobe thought he could have extramarital affairs and not pay a dear and devastating price. Obviously, the aforementioned individuals—and many, many others—who have made such self-destructive and self-sabotaging decisions were dead wrong.

This chapter isn't meant to be preachy or moralistic. It's about being ever-cognizant of the hard, cold reality that when making your decisions, if you play with fire, you may very well get burned—and depending upon the severity of those burns, they may never go away.

Strata-Gems:

- When making your decisions, be aware that you can accomplish many positive things, but one egregious act or mistake—made knowingly or unknowingly—can tarnish and/or wipe away all the good that you've done, and can irreparably damage you and those around you.

- Avoid even the appearance of impropriety, because perception, in some instances, can be as damaging as reality.

- It is crucial in constructive decision-making that you carefully and objectively consider and visually picture the risks and consequences of your decisions *before* you act. Additionally, honestly evaluate the possible damage versus the possible benefits of your decisions. If you do this, it may well save you from making a costly mistake or misstep.

TIMING, APPROPRIATENESS, AND
RELATIVITY

You've probably heard the saying, "There's a time and a place for everything." This can be phrased another way: "What might be appropriate behavior in one circumstance might be totally inappropriate in another."

In life, there's a time to be disciplined and to delay gratification, as well as a time to be spontaneous and to go for the immediate gratification or solution. There's a time to be focused and a time to relax. There's a time to look and plan ahead, and a time to enjoy the moment and the process.

"Appropriateness" is a relative concept that is wholly dependent upon context. The key is to grow to understand and to master the concept of appropriateness by being a *Student of Life* and by being a keen observer of people and their behaviors in particular. Both appropriateness and timing are essential components of healthy and constructive decision-making. Acting appropriately or inappropriately, and having good timing or poor timing, can profoundly impact the quality of your life and your professional and personal relationships.

Individuals who have a track record of accomplishments either innately possess or, through forethought, experience, and preparation, have developed good instincts about the timing and appropriateness of their decisions and actions. People who don't succeed as often may be less proficient judges of what is appropriate behavior at a given time or in a given context. They may not execute their actions correctly, even if their choice of behavior and its timing are correct. Individuals who are self-destructive and who sabotage themselves and their personal and professional relationships are quite adept at choosing the wrong or inappropriate strategies for any given occasion—and it's not by accident, no matter what they claim. The negative forces that dwell within and guide them are pretty savvy.

As human beings, we all have different sides. The issue that faces all of us is: What is the most appropriate time and occasion to express a particular side? As structured as I am, I also love being spontaneous and romantic. As health and fitness conscious as I am, there are times when I find it absolutely appropriate to go off my diet. It all depends upon what's appropriate in a particular context.

As a case in point, I remind you here of an earlier story in which my client, Julianna, when she was asked whether she would postpone her vacation in order to fill in for someone whose position she aspired to attain, weighed the different components and values of the situation. I believe that Julianna correctly weighed her values and concluded that it was the appropriate time to stay and anchor, and the inappropriate time to take her vacation and thereby allow her competition for this job to fill in. Both Julianna and I calculated that it would be a more appropriate time to take her vacation sometime after the main anchor job was filled by her, or by someone else.

In the upcoming chapter about subjectivity, I will recount two instances in which I had the chance to postpone my education in order to take advantage of two different time-sensitive opportunities. In one case, I chose not to postpone my education. In the other, I did. My decisions were based upon concepts of timing and appropriateness, when taken in the context of the specific situation at hand.

Always keep in mind that timing and appropriateness are not absolutes. They are relative terms. The timing and appropriateness of any behavior must always be judged in the context of your value system, your goals (which should reflect your highest values), and the unique situation that you are dealing with.

Therefore, when you're deciding the timing of an act, or its appropriateness, you must examine these factors in conjunction with all of the *Crunch Time Strategies, Strata-Gems,* and other elements that will factor into your decisions. Just as Julianna decided that forgoing her vacation at that particular time was appropriate and wise behavior, she might well have reached a completely different decision at a different time and under different circumstances.

Strata-Gem:

There's a time and a place for different decisions. Which decision is appropriate at a particular time or in a particular context is dependent upon what you value most, the unique situation at hand, and your goals at the time.

PRE–CRUNCH TIME DECISION-MAKING
The Power of Proactivity, Preparation, and Practice

Two absolutely essential components of great decision-making are *proactivity* and *preparation*. Let's study them, beginning with their definitions:

> *Proactivity:* acting in anticipation of future problems, needs, or changes.*
>
> *Preparation:* the action or process of . . . getting ready for some occasion, test, or duty.**
>
> [To] *Prepare*: to make ready beforehand for some purpose, use, or activity . . . to put in the proper state of mind; to plan in advance.***

By being a proactive decision-maker, you both identify and anticipate that there will be future problems, needs, opportunities, questions, temptations, etc., that you may or will have to deal with at some point in the future. By engaging in effective and thorough preparation, and putting yourself in a proper state of mind before you are faced with having to make a decision regarding some problem, need, temptation, opportunity, question, etc., you are creating

*Merriam-Webster's Collegiate Dictionary, Tenth Ed., p. 928
**Merriam-Webster's Collegiate Dictionary, Tenth Ed., p. 920
***Merriam-Webster's Collegiate Dictionary, Tenth Ed., p. 920

ting one of the most constructive and self-enhancing
lable for raising both the quality of your life and your
f-esteem.

rtant components of being proactive and preparatory
are that you, in advance, are able to identify your potential temptations, weaknesses, vices, "fatal attractions," blind spots, cravings, ad-
dictions, etc., and you are able to proactively devise a plan of action
that you will not, for any reason, deviate from when faced with any
temptation, or other attractive alternatives or options. Please remember that this type of ironclad, pre–*Crunch Time* decision-making is
only wise and effective if you accept the condition that there will be
absolutely no reason for you to reexamine your options at *Crunch
Time*, because there will be no circumstances, unforeseen or otherwise,
that will make an alternate decision the right or the better thing to do.

For example, I remember Dr. Art Ulene saying on the *Today* show
that in order to give up smoking, "You must plan ahead of time. Also,
you must know [ahead of time] what you're going to do in a crisis period." In essence, you must preplan *your* responses (consistent with
your highest priorities and values and most cherished goals), and res-
olutely stick with them, no matter what or how strong the urge is to
deviate from your preplanned decisions.

For example, let's discuss how proactive, pre–*Crunch Time* decision-
making could have significantly changed Kobe Bryant's life for the better.
Kobe could have anticipated and acknowledged that as a star professional athlete and a highly recognizable public figure, many opportunities of all sorts will come his way. Some of these opportunities may at
first appear attractive and/or enticing but when examined in the context
of the *Big Picture* of his life and his most cherished values, they will ultimately be inappropriate and non-self-enhancing, or worse, destructive
or poisonous courses of action.

He could have identified the numerous blessings and gifts that he
enjoys, such as his beautiful wife, new child, potential Hall of Fame
basketball career, numerous lucrative endorsements, peace of mind,
and the respect and adulation of basketball fans and non-basketball
fans alike, which he would never want to lose or jeopardize losing.

He could have taken an honest look at his potential emotional weaknesses or needs, and if he sensed that there were any possibility that the temptation to have extramarital sex could be a potentially overwhelming urge, he could have acknowledged it and taken strong, appropriate steps to protect himself against making a destructive and an extremely costly decision.

He could have visualized getting caught and the horrible feelings and devastating consequences that he and his loved ones would suffer as a result of his bad decision. Since consequences count, in every instance, it is imperative that they are focused on and prominently factored into decision-making equations.

He could have preplanned his decision not to risk his wonderful life and golden future by letting an emotional/sexual urge—no matter how strong—or an emotional weakness—no matter how overwhelming—lead to a self-destructive and poisonous decision at *Crunch Time*. No how! No way.

He could have *taken appropriate steps to insure* that he wouldn't make a destructive decision at *Crunch Time* by doing the following

1) *Framing*™ the issue before him in such a way that he would surely be compelled to make a self-enhancing decision.* He could accomplish this by tapping into one of his deepest and most powerful emotions (such as the fear of the loss of all of the great things that he now enjoys; or the fear of unbearable, worldwide humiliation for him and his family if he were caught committing adultery or, worse, convicted of rape). The powerful emotional force of fear and being fully cognizant of the horrific consequences would hopefully override, vitiate, and counteract the carnal urge.

For example, he could have pre-*framed* his decision this way: "No matter how great or alluring the opportunity is to have an extramarital romance or sexual relations, it's just not worth risking all I have, all I've

---

*The concept of "framing" a decision is discussed in greater depth in Step 6.

worked so hard to achieve, and all I can have in the future, for an hour or two of physical gratification with a woman I don't even know or can trust. Nor do I want to risk humiliating myself and all those who love and care about me. I'm smarter than that! I'm not that self-destructive. I'm not that weak! So I'll just turn my back on it. I must take great pains to be strong and resolute in my excellent decision to stay clear of this poisonous situation and any others that come my way."

2) Not putting himself in vulnerable positions (such as flirting with women or inviting them to his hotel room). The constructive move here would have been for Kobe to put the percentages in his favor, so that he wouldn't allow himself to be faced with a tough, emotionally-charged decision because he proactively decided not to put himself in harm's way. Constructive decision-makers know that if they don't play with fire (and don't even have matches or lighters around), they significantly increase their chances that they'll never get burned.

He could have made and implemented the self-enhancing decision to ignore or sidestep his urges and needs, by recognizing that this was a red-flag temptation, and as a result, consciously and deliberately not pay any attention to the young woman when he met her. Kobe could have accomplished this by sticking to his preplanned, emotionally charged, *framed* decision at *Crunch Time*, and by once again reminding himself of all his many gifts and blessings.

He could have stayed clear of the woman in question, and then inwardly savored, applauded, and celebrated his great, self-enhancing behavior. By positively reinforcing his decision-making triumph, he could have raised both the level of his self-esteem and his feelings of self-worth, which in turn would have fueled him to make more and more constructive decisions in the future.

Finally, he could have practiced making enhancing, preplanned decisions thereafter. By doing this, his constructive reactions, actions, and decisions would hopefully become reflexive, just as they are on a basketball court. As Kobe unquestionably knows, with focused practice and repetition of the right moves comes near-perfect execution at *Crunch Time*.

It is my belief that Kobe never took the time to honestly consider what the real and devastating consequences would be, nor did he try to objectively delineate and weigh the overwhelming potential negatives versus the very minimal positives of the temptation that he was faced with, when reviewed in the context of the *Big Picture* of his personal and professional life. I am also convinced that he gave no consideration as to how it would really feel to be publicly humiliated, excoriated, and vilified. Forewarned is forearmed. *Framing* the issue before him would have helped him to meet and conquer one of the most important challenges of his life. His circumstances clearly illustrate the great danger of being mentally and emotionally *unprepared* to deal with certain opportunities and/or temptations that we may be subject to.

In connection with Kobe's basketball endeavors, everything I've heard or read tells me that he has carefully thought out, anticipated, and constructively prepared for just about anything that might come his way during the heat of competition. If he had just as constructively, thoroughly, and tenaciously prepared to avoid personal self-destructive temptations and behaviors—and practiced this diligently—in all likelihood he would not have made his very costly mistake.

Proactive, preplanned decisions can make all the positive difference in the world when you or your loved ones are introduced and/or required to respond to a specific unhealthy or potentially dangerous stimulus. For example, when cigarettes, recreational drugs, alcohol, or the opportunity to engage in any activity or relationship that you feel is wrong or dangerous is offered to you.

Let's go back to the chapter on "Constructively Acting—Not Reacting—When Faced With A Decision," where I discussed that prior to playing Mike Smith (the tennis opponent who distracted me with his antics) a second time, I preplanned my ironclad response to whatever he might try in our upcoming match. That response was: *I will ignore anything distracting that he tries, and focus on playing the best tennis I was capable of.* As you know, this pre-*Crunch Time* decision-making worked wonderfully, as I defeated my very talented opponent that day.

I've done the same thing when I've attended parties or events where cigarettes and recreational drugs have been offered to me. My preplanned mental response was, "No how, no way." I articulated this pre–*Crunch Time* decision as, "No, thanks. We athletes have to stay in tip-top shape."

For years, I've had a preplanned response to being offered desserts and sweets: "No, thank you. I was fat once, and I never want to be fat again. But I appreciate the offer. I'll just have some fruit (or whatever is around that's not fattening)."

If you remember one piece of information from this book, remember that if you can:

1) Identify what you truly want for and in your life (and also what you don't want);
2) Clearly and wisely *preplan* your decisions accordingly; and
3) Stick with those decisions at *Crunch Time* (which is made easier to do by compellingly *framing* them);

you have given yourself the very best chance to achieve your most cherished goals and truly live your dreams.

"Evolved Thinking"—More Pre–*Crunch Time* Decision-Making

One of the most healthy and "evolved" ways of thinking is to reason things through and proactively choose a healthy and wise course of action *before* you are faced with a negative or positive occurrence.

In Dr. Deepak Chopra's book *Unconditional Life*, he recounts the story of a female attorney who worked herself to death so that she could attain a certain salary and position by the time she reached the age of forty. And once she attained these goals, she would then take the time to smell the roses and enjoy her family and professional achievements. But just as she reached her goals, she was diagnosed with terminal cancer. Curiously, when the doctor advised her of her illness, she said that she experienced a great deal of "liberation." She felt "happy." The disease forced her to get out of the rat race—which, deep down, she had always wanted to do and knew she should do—and to finally savor every day of the rest of her life. As she put it, "Cancer allowed me to achieve my final goal. To retire at forty."

As Dr. Chopra observes, "Disease is no way to solve the core issues of life." You don't need to experience something terrible or irreparable to force or catalyze you to do something that, in your heart and soul, you *know* you need to do for your psychological, emotional, and spiritual well-being.

Why is it that so many people in our society have to nearly destroy themselves before they do healthy and constructive things? And once they see the light and get on the right track, they may not find themselves with enough time or the right circumstances to enjoy the life that now, suddenly, seems so worth living and cherishing.

Truly wise decision-making requires, and healthy self-love dictates, that you decide to do constructive and self-enhancing things *before* you have to experience a dangerous and/or destructive lesson. Prior to embarking on a course of action, proactively think what the wise, healthy, and higher thing to do is. And then do it. Follow your *Heart-of-Hearts* and your inner voices, the ones that tell you not to do the easy or popular thing of the day or the moment, but to instead pursue the constructive and enhancing course of action when seen in the context of the *Big Picture* of your life. Even if it's not always fun or easy!

In the film *Damage*, a father (Jeremy Irons) secretly dates his son's girlfriend. This father engaged in behavior that was obviously wrong. As we discussed earlier, if you continually play with fire, eventually you'll get burned. Eventually, his son is accidentally killed after he finds his father being intimate with his girlfriend. As a result, the father loses his job; his wife, who is emotionally devastated, leaves him; and the girl with whom he was having the affair also leaves. In the bone-chilling closing shot of the film, the father is seen sitting on the floor in the corner of the room, knees bent up against his chest, rocking back and forth . . . *alone*. Because of his selfishness and thoughtlessness, he and everyone around him were damaged in a most profound and irreparable way.

You only have one life to live. You can decide to make it great. You can proactively choose to enhance yourself and lift others. Or you can compromise yourself, the truth, your potential, and your life. You can choose to play with fire, and damage yourself and all those you touch. As to what decision-making strategies you adopt and act out, the choice is yours to make!

On the flip side, I remember a very special day in September, 1969. The "miracle" New York Mets, for the first time in their young history, had reached first place in the National League East standings. On that day, in the New York *Daily News*, there was a full page cigarette ad opposite the baseball standings that read: "Isn't this a Camel Moment?" It was truly a great day and an all-too-memorable ad.

I've always felt that what that advertisement implicitly said was: "We've waited a long time for this major event. Let's celebrate. Let's enjoy. Savor the moment with a Camel."

In the film *Waiting to Exhale*, the strategy for three of the four leading women was: "Unless and until I find a husband, I'll be praying and holding my breath. And once I find him, I can thank God, relax, and exhale."

In both of these instances, accomplishing a greatly desired or valued goal (the Mets reaching first place and someone finding a husband), would trigger a perceived positive reaction (lighting up a Camel and finally exhaling). But just as you shouldn't wait to hit "rock bottom" before you (through your decisions) raise the quality of your life and appreciate the greatness of living, you should also not wait for great events, or the passing of predetermined time frames, to raise the quality of your decision-making and your feelings of self-esteem and self-worth. Instead, start today to make constructive decisions!

Unlike the female attorney who was diagnosed with terminal cancer, take the time—before you are shaken out of your ruts and defenses—to smell each and every rose, by making constructive decisions *before* you're forced to.

When you think that you're having a bad day at the office, at home, or in the car while stuck in traffic, think again. Look at the *Big Picture*. Being told that you have terminal cancer or losing someone you love can make for a really bad day. Don't let the other stuff take your attention away from cherishing and enjoying every moment of your life. Think about it: When you're on your deathbed, will you only then realize how silly you were to get aggravated and be angry about things that in the *Big Picture* you can barely remember and really meant nothing? We have precious little time on Earth. Constructive decision-making dictates that you begin to exhale and make every moment a "*Camel-less* moment" as soon as possible.

If you can proactively decide to raise the level of your life *before* you learn a costly lesson, and if you can proactively decide to make the most of each day that you're alive and not wait for some artificial time frame to pass or some event to take place, you will indeed be wiser, healthier, and happier, and a highly evolved decision-maker.

The day that my life changed immeasurably for the better was the day that I began to *take ownership* of my decisions and my actions. It was when I took an honest external look at myself, embarked upon an internal exploration into my *Heart-of-Hearts*, and tapped into how I really felt that I knew that I was unhappy with myself and my lot in life in a few key areas. Being overweight—and feeling badly about it— was one of them. I realized that I had to change. I would do this by raising the level of my thinking and acting, by taking responsibility for myself, and by being more disciplined than I had been in the past. Pre-planned constructive decisions helped me to accomplish this.

My life indeed changed that day. However, the point at which the quality of my life was truly enhanced for all time was when I began to make constructive decisions and do enhancing things for myself and others, *before* I had to, *before* I was forced to, or *before* it was too late.

Performing positive and healthy acts *before* you reach rock-bottom or *before* a great event happens is often easier to accomplish (because you don't have to make up for so much lost time or damage), and it's often more fun and gratifying.

If you want to attain your goals and enhance your life, the *Strategy* of being an evolved and a proactive thinker is crucial to your success.

Seize the day—and all the rest of your days—with proactive, evolved decision-making and behavior.

Strata Gems:

- There are some instances when it is appropriate for you to decide to preplan your actions and not engage in any further strategy examination when a stimulus is presented to you. These are situations in which there will be no way that a modification of your preplanned decision will result in a healthier or more enhancing outcome.

- One of your most constructive *Strategies* is to practice making positive and healthy decisions, and implement them *before* something bad or good happens to you. This is evolved and self-enhancing pre–*Crunch Time* thinking, strategizing, and behavior.

IF YOU DO THE RIGHT THINGS, THE RIGHT THINGS WILL HAPPEN

In many ways, the core premise of our journey is: If you do the right things, the right things will happen. Or, put another way: If you make constructive, wise, and enhancing minor and major decisions, positive results will more than likely come your way. Why? Because you're putting yourself in the right position and stacking the percentages in your favor for you to reap the benefits of your good decision-making. For example, here are just some of the individuals we've discussed who have fulfilled their dreams by making constructive, wise, and empowering decisions.

- My dad, when he decided to keep himself in top physical and mental shape after he was "retired" by his former employer. Three years later, he got an opportunity to begin a new career at age sixty-nine. Twenty-seven years later, he's still working.

- My client, Julianna, who decided to forgo her vacation and be a fill-in anchor. Due in large part to her constructive decision-making, she was offered the anchor job that she coveted.

- My client who decided to stay positive and constructive after being publicly embarrassed by a demotion to a lesser anchor position. His constructive behavior enabled him to secure a wonderful anchor job in a top market.

- My client, Dayna Devon, who underperformed during her local market interview but then constructively learned from her experience. Months later, with an arsenal of modified interviewing and auditioning strategies, she was offered a once-in-a-lifetime host position on the show of her dreams.

- I was able to secure the representation of some excellent broadcast journalists at pivotal junctures in their careers and in mine by being appropriately creative, proactive, and spontaneous.

I can fill books with stories of my clients and others whom I know who, by doing the right things (e.g., making constructive decisions), made great things happen for themselves.

Please remember that not every constructive decision will lead to a great result. Sometimes, as we've discussed, things aren't always meant to be, and something better, different, or more appropriate may happen instead. But take heart—throughout my years of counseling experience, I've seen incontrovertible evidence, time and time again, that if you make constructive decisions and implement them correctly, good and great things usually do happen.

Strata-Gem:

If you do the right, wise, and constructive thing, good and/or great things will often happen for you.

OBJECTIVITY—LOOKING AT
THINGS HONESTLY

One of the gifts that I received from playing tennis and paddle tennis is the understanding and appreciation of the fact that I must look at my defeats and triumphs, and my flaws and strengths, honestly. Pre-match preparation (pre–*Crunch Time* decision-making), the gathering and assimilation of data during a match (*Crunch Time* decision-making), and post-match reflection and study (post–*Crunch Time* decision-making), all require honesty.

I know that if I'm to improve on the court, I must be able to objectively see and examine what I've done right, what I've done wrong, and learn from both.

When studying what I've done wrong or could have done better, my goal is to take my "cerebral tweezers," pluck out the problem or flaw, decide how I could have handled things differently, more appropriately, and/or more constructively, and then incorporate the most efficacious choice and behavior into my decision-making and behavioral repertoires for the future.

In becoming the best decision-maker possible, you must strive to see things and understand people for what and who they really are. Don't be defensive about your mistakes or shortcomings. Don't view things as you'd like them to be or wish they could be. You have to deal with what's *real*. If you've made a mistake, acknowledge it, accept it, and correct it. Mistakes and missteps are part of life. Everyone makes them. The key is to not make the same mistakes over and over again because you consciously or subconsciously choose not to make the effort to objectively review and study your decisions and behavior.

In order to become the wisest and most enhancing decision-maker possible, you must be your own scientist, and the elements in your decision-making equation must be the pure, real, unadulterated truth.

The next *Strategies* focus on helping you to discern what is *real* and *true*.

SUBJECTIVITY AND UNDERSTANDING
WHERE OTHERS ARE COMING FROM

As I think about my law school experience, I vividly remember the day in our constitutional law class that I learned about the "legislative history" of a law. That is, the modification and edification process that a proposed law goes through in the Senate and the House of Representatives before it is finally passed. From the legislative history of the law, we can ascertain the "why," the "what," and the "how" of a law. In essence, we learn how to correctly interpret the law by understanding why the law was originally introduced and ultimately passed; why it is drafted as it is; what the law is supposed to accomplish; and how the law is intended to be administered. So knowing the legislative history of a law enables us to understand it by, in essence, understanding where it's coming from.

It's the same thing with people. If you understand where they're coming from—their personal values, opinions, likes, and dislikes—you may interpret what you are seeing and/or hearing more accurately, and thus be a more effective decision-maker in regard to those individuals.

For example, the other day, the general manager at the station where a very talented and successful client of mine works called me. He said that he had just watched my client on the air, and that he "hated" her hairstyle and clothes. When I related this information to my client, she expressed exasperation with her boss, explaining, "I just went to the best hairstylist in Manhattan and I just finished spending a fortune at Brooks Brothers on some new clothes. He just doesn't appreciate anything." I then took a few moments to explain to my client why I thought her decision-making was flawed. "Before you get your hair cut and go clothes shopping next time," I told her, "have a conversation with your G.M. Ask him what *he* wants, because he's the one that you're trying to please. Think of it this way—if you bring him Chinese food and he hates Chinese food, most of the time you won't secure the desired positive response. However, if you know what he wants and know what will make him happy, and you base your decisions on those preferences, you will greatly increase the chance that your decisions will be received in a positive way."

That said, if you know and understand the individual around whom your decision revolves and use this knowledge and understanding correctly, you are likely to make a constructive and wise decision. I also counsel my clients that life *is* like a Rorschach test. Everyone brings his or her own perceptions, life experiences, and beliefs to the table when perceiving and interpreting the "inkblots"—or life events.

For example, a woman named Claire entered a wedding reception that was already underway. She headed directly for her seat at Table 28, and didn't stop to make eye contact with anyone. While I was standing at the buffet table, I heard three different takes on Claire's entrance. One woman said, "Look at Claire Wilson. She thinks she's better than all of us. The 'princess' just walks in and glides to her table. She didn't even smile back at those she passed. *Boy, is she cold and stuck-up.*" A second woman said, "There's Claire. God, she's so beautiful, but she doesn't even know it. *She's so shy.* If I don't go over and introduce her to people, she'll never have the confidence to do it herself." While a guy standing nearby said, "Did you see Claire walk in here? *She's doing everything she can to avoid me.* I don't know what I did to piss her off."

As it turned out, Claire's best friend had been in a car accident the day before, and Claire's thoughts as she entered the reception were all about that friend. *Will she live? If she does, will she be paralyzed?* In honor of her cousin's marriage, Claire showed up at the wedding, left quickly, and rejoined her friend at the hospital.

The manner in which Claire entered the reception was interpreted in three different ways by three different individuals. All of them brought their own unique set of experiences, values, perceptions, insecurities, defenses, needs, and more to the interpretation. As a result, Claire was perceived as a "snob," as "shy," and as "angry." That evening, she was none of these things. She was preoccupied.

Because individuals can and do see identical things in such diverse ways, their *subjective* reality can have a material impact upon how they interact with others. It is crucial that you integrate this reality into your decision-making equations. Here are some examples and thoughts on the subject.

Our Expectations Won't Always Be Met— "Anticipointments"

Since different people understand and value things differently than you do, they can and do perceive things differently. Because of this, people reach different decisions and act differently than you would in a given circumstance. So if you have expectations, and you anticipate that others will act in a certain way, you may well be disappointed, hurt, or angry when they don't. Or, as some say, you may be "anticipointed."

For example, I remember making a date to go for a bike ride with a friend and to spend the rest of that Sunday with her. She told me to give her a call on Sunday morning to figure out a time and place to meet. I called and called on Sunday, but repeatedly got her answering machine. Finally, at 3:30 that afternoon, she left a message saying that something had come up and she couldn't make it. When I eventually spoke with her the next day, I learned that when she made a date, it meant, "Let's think about it, and if we're still in the mood, we'll figure it out. If not, we'll just hang loose and do it some other time. No big deal."

In this scenario, we were working from the same word, "date," but we were working under very different interpretations. I perceived a date as something etched in stone unless something urgent happened. I made my plans around the commitment of a date. My emotions were stirred by the expectation of the date. I was looking forward to it. However, my friend perceived a date as something much looser. Something between a possibility and a probability—but by no means a firm commitment.

Was I hurt that she attached so little value to the time that she could have spent with me? Yes! Was I angry that I had planned my day around being with her, and that she was so cavalier about blowing it off? You bet. Why? Because according to my value system, if I value a person, I look forward to and keep the date. Therefore, I inferred that I must not be very valuable to her. But what I learned is that *I must put myself in the other person's shoes when trying to interpret and understand where he or she is coming from.*

After discussing the incident with her, I learned that she did value me, but that she had always been relaxed about her social time. If the date happens, cool. If not, cool. "It's no big deal." As we spent more time together, I learned that she had experienced a pretty rough childhood. Her father, whom she dearly loved, had abandoned her and her family. Different guys came in and out of her mom's life. Apparently, no one stayed for very long. There had never been a lot of continuity in her life. I began to understand that my friend's behavior was her way of coping with having had her expectations unfulfilled and frustrated many times during her childhood. Her behavior, in essence, said: "I have no expectations. You should have no expectations. And no one—especially me—gets disappointed or hurt (again)."

I learned that her cavalier behavior wasn't about me at all. It was all about her and the strategy with which she chose to protect herself, after being let down so many times during her early years. Once I understood all of this, and therefore where she was coming from, I was no longer hurt and angry about her treatment of me.

I eventually explained to her my perspective of our date. I said that I considered a date to be a firm commitment, and that I had very much looked forward to, and planned my Sunday around, spending time with her. My decision not to make any other plans on that Sunday was based on this perspective. I also explained that my time was precious to me, and that I believed one should respect another person's time. In our case, my Sunday was wasted waiting to hear from her, because I couldn't make alternate plans. After our discussion, my friend and I reached an agreement: When we make a date, it is for real, unless something unforeseeable happens. For the past five years, she has kept all but one of our dates. I have done my best to never cancel—and disappoint her.

The lesson I learned was that *everyone makes decisions according to his or her own unique past experiences, values, and perceptions of the world.* People *do* see and value things differently. If you want to be as successful as possible in your relationships, and if you desire to be a wiser decision-maker, you need to be fully cognizant of the differences that exist in peoples' values, perceptions, and interpretations. You need to be open and sensitive to these differences. By doing so, you will be less likely to hurt, disappoint and/or anger others, because you hopefully will take others' perspectives into account when choosing a course of action. You will also be better able to understand why others don't always see things or treat you the way you would like or expect them to.

In essence, if you clearly understand that different people can and do perceive the same things differently, you will be much more effective in responsively and constructively dealing with your own expectations and those of others when drawing your conclusions and/or reaching your decisions.

Understanding Subjectivity

One thing that I've learned in broadcasting is that there's no accounting for taste. I remember an evening when a friend invited me to a dinner party attended by her family and their friends, all of whom were from Pittsburgh. My friend told everyone at the table that I represented newscasters, and that a number of my clients were television anchors and reporters in their city. As a result, for the next hour I heard why one person loved anchor "x," and two people couldn't watch him; why three people loved anchor "y," but my friend's mother found her "cold;" and why four people loved the "hip" way one young anchor dressed, while two others felt that she didn't look or dress like a *journalist*. Like the story about Claire, who walked into the wedding reception, everyone brought his or her own subjective taste to the table (literally). Once again, this was prima facie evidence that people see and react to the same stimuli differently.

However, I've decided that subjectivity is a phenomenon that I can live with. If all women liked one person, I'd *never* get a date. Or, if all newscasters found one agent desirable—and that agent wasn't me—I'd be out of business. So I'll take the good with the bad. Since everyone has different tastes, I'll win some—or many—but not every one.

Because of the very personal psychological dynamics of subjectivity, not everyone will like a given person. Not everyone will see how smart they are, how talented they are, or that they are the best at what they do. It's impossible to please everyone. This is a crucial concept and a clear reality that I remind my clients of all the time. It should also be said that the reasons for the lack of approval or rejection may have nothing at all to do with the individuals being evaluated, and everything to do with the evaluator.

For example, I eventually learned that one of my clients didn't sign with me years earlier because the first time she saw me, she thought that I was a "weasel." When I asked her why she felt that way, she said, "Because you *looked* like one." (I later learned that I actually looked like someone with whom she had had a bad experience years earlier.) Recently, after securing her representation and getting her numerous network and top-market offers, she happily accepted a great position and a wonderful deal in her hometown. Figuring that I had won her over, I confidently asked, *"Now* do you still think that I'm a weasel?" She replied, "Yep . . . but you're an *effective* one!"

There is a simple but eloquent prayer that goes like this: "God, grant me the serenity to accept the things that I cannot change, the courage to change the things I can, and the wisdom to know the difference." In life, there are times when we just can't win someone over, when they *just don't get it*, no matter how much we think they should. Not everyone got The Beatles when they were hot. Not everyone likes Elvis, or *Friends*, or *Sex and the City*. Some just don't get it. You will be much wiser and happier if you know up front that not everyone will get you, your points of view, or your values.

No One Gets it Right All of the Time

If there are so many experts, why do Las Vegas casinos flourish? Why do bookies stay in business? Why do people "in the know" lose money on Wall Street? Why are some children of psychiatrists and psychologists emotionally screwed up? Why? Because no one is always right. No one always does everything correctly, no matter how smart or talented he or she appears to be. No matter what their status, position, or reputation.

No one always makes the right decision or always knows the correct solution or course of action in connection with each unique situation. Therefore, a critical element of constructive decision-making is *how we value the subjective input of others*. Some *Strategies* that I share with my clients are:

- The subjective perceptions, values, and advice of one person may not always be right for another individual in a given instance, and must not be followed without careful examination and evaluation.

- When reaching a decision, it's important to accurately assess how much weight to accord certain advice, approval, and criticism. This largely depends upon who is giving it, the arena in which the advice is given (e.g., is the person qualified in this particular area?), and what the advice-giver's agendas, fears, motives, etc., might be for giving the advice, approval, or criticism.

- Since everyone can be wrong, after you follow the *Eight Crunch Time Steps*, don't be afraid to make a tough decision, trust your instincts, and/or take worthwhile risks.

- Parents or significant and/or esteemed others don't have all the answers; they are human and fallible, just as we are. When this is truly understood, the once awesome disparity between perceived perfect parents and fallible children may be put in a more realistic perspective. This makes it easier to modify old strategies that have been based upon parents' and key caretakers' hallowed opinions, beliefs, behaviors, and expectations (for you).

On that note, I'd like to share a couple of relevant stories with you.

By the time my dad was fourteen, he was working full time to help support his family. In a true Horatio Alger scenario, he progressed from a stock boy to executive vice president of a prominent department store chain. However, he always felt insecure about the fact that he didn't have the formal education that those above, around, and below him at his company had. There were times when my dad had offers to join other companies, and had backers who wanted him to strike out on his own. However, he chose to stay with his company because security was of the greatest importance and value to him. As a result, he wasn't inclined to take any significant professional risks.

In my sophomore year of college, I had a chance to be coached by Gardner Malloy, a former world-class tennis champion, and to play the international tennis circuit. The hitch was that I would have to quit college and play tennis full time. When I told my dad about my opportunity, he froze with fear and anger.

He couldn't talk. His son was now at *Harvard*, and would almost certainly have great prospects and a secure life upon graduation. This was more than my father could have ever hoped for. After an endless moment, he responded angrily, "You've got it all going for you. Are you going to throw it all away to be a tennis bum? Do you want to teach tennis the rest of your life under the hot sun, and dry up like a prune?"

He walked away in apparent disgust. I believe that my dad was scared to death that I would make a horrible life decision. For about a week, he couldn't talk to me. Gardner Malloy suggested that I could always go back to school later, but when it comes to athletics, I had to give it my best shot while I was still young. He was right. Gardner concluded by saying, "Before you reach your decision, you should remember one thing: It's the things that you never do that you'll always regret." I believe that he was somewhat right on this one. I've been invited to go bungee jumping a couple of times. I've declined, and I don't regret it. However, all in all, this was pretty heavy and heady stuff for a nineteen-year-old to be deciding. Since my mom was sensitive to my love of athletics and the need to go for it while you're young, she said that she would support me in whatever I chose—as long as I thought things out carefully and clearly.

I did. I acknowledged that I was really starting to enjoy my pre-law studies as much as, or more than, I enjoyed playing tennis. My priorities seemed to be changing. I was very excited about writing my senior thesis on decision-making. I had also experienced ligament problems in one of my ankles in recent years. I wasn't sure that my body would have been able to withstand the grueling punishment of practicing and competing every day. And when I got right down to it, in my *Heart-of-Hearts*, I knew that no matter how good I was as a tennis player, I didn't think I'd become good enough to enjoy consistent success at the top level of the pro tour.

On the other hand, athletics had been my life. They were inextricably intertwined with my identity and my sense of self. Athletics, for the most part, helped me change from being a heavy, clumsy, insecure child, to a thinner, more agile, accomplished young adult. Being an athlete made me stand out—it made me special. I liked Gardner's idea of going back to school if things didn't work out, or even if they did. What a free and exciting way to live, playing tennis all over the world, being coached for a year or so by world-renowned Gardner Malloy.

It sounded great . . . but it didn't sound *right*.

On the last day of my two-week trip to Florida, Gardner and I played an exhibition match at the Fontainebleau Hotel, where he was the director of tennis. After just two weeks of playing tennis full time and being coached by Gardner, my game rose almost two levels. I felt as though I was playing some of the best tennis of my life. I continued to play well, as I started the exhibition match by jumping off to a quick lead.

Then suddenly, it all caved in. I had to face what my final decision *had* to be. I was going back to school. Later that day, I would leave the sunny skies and eighty-degree weather of Miami Beach to return to snowy, cold Cambridge, Massachusetts, to catch up and study for final exams. There would be no more intense practice sessions coached by Gardner. Studying would once again take clear priority. Within days of returning to school, my game would inevitably begin to slip. For the next four weeks or so, I could, at best, play an hour or two of tennis a couple of times each week. That's no way to raise your game. Gardner's words came crashing through my mind, *"It's the things that you never do that you'll always regret."* I began to lose track of the exhibition match. If I wasn't crying on the outside, I certainly was within. I didn't win another game the rest of the match. I couldn't stand to see myself playing well, because I knew it would all be for naught.

That evening, Gardner drove me to the airport. He could tell that I had made up my mind. As we parted, he gave me a copy of the book he wrote, *A Will to Win*. In it he inscribed his prophetic words, "It's the things . . ."

As I boarded the plane to Cambridge, I knew that I had just closed the door on the most sacred and cherished part of my life: the beauty, passion, and pure innocence of seriously pursuing athletics.

On the plane, as I thumbed through Gardner's book, I reflected on the fact that I had reached my decision not because of the pressure put on me by my dad, but because of my own heartfelt reasons. Earlier that day, I had told my parents of my decision. My dad was thrilled, and I truly understood why. My mom wanted to be sure that I was comfortable with my decision. She asked if I was sad. I said that I was, but that I had made the right choice.

However, it was not until two years later that I learned a huge lesson. It was the night that I played my first match against Arthur Ashe—and won. After the match, my dad walked up to me, kissed and hugged me, and said, "Maybe you *should* have played professional tennis."

So many things ran through my mind at that moment! Things like, "Oh, *now* I get it. You didn't want me to pursue tennis because you didn't think that I was good enough." And, "Great! Two years later, when I no longer have Gardner to coach me and I've lost two unrecoverable years of development, you start to have an open mind!"

But upon reflection, I came to the following conclusions. First, I *know* that my dad really loves me, but I also now know that he saw things through his subjective eyes—eyes that valued security over almost anything else. Because he often feared that he might not be good enough, he feared that I, too, might not be good enough. He feared that I would throw everything away—everything that I (and he) had worked for. *But his values may not coincide with my values.* From now on, when listening to his advice, I must always take this into account.

I also realize that had I decided not to pursue tennis full time because I would have incurred my dad's disapproval, I would have been devastated after beating Arthur Ashe and hearing him say, "Maybe you should have gone for it." The lesson that I learned and the goal to strive for is *to make decisions based on values that I can live with, because I am the one who has to live with them for the rest of my life.* I realized in that instance that my dad's and mom's perspectives aren't always right for me. And, as I get older and grow wiser about myself, there will be times when I'm going to have to make decisions that they won't agree with. And I will—because sometimes "*child* knows best!" (what's in his or her own *Heart-of-Hearts*).

I also realized that I had reached the right decision (not to pursue tennis in lieu of attending college) two years earlier when my victory over Ashe and my dad's remark didn't make me second-guess myself. My decision had been based upon good reasoning and an accurate perception of where my true interests and priorities were heading.

As we grow up, we all are subject to expectations put on us by our parents or primary caregivers, friends, teachers, loved ones, employers, etc. I learned that when reaching my decisions, I must not let those expectations lead me to make flawed or destructive decisions. It's wonderful to live up to, or exceed, someone's or society's expectations, but only if my decisions and actions are healthy and constructive for me in my life.

When dealing with the burden of expectations, I must continually examine them, test them, and see whether they are constructive and uniquely right for me to live up to and set as benchmarks. If they are, great. If not, I must set myself free of them and choose wiser and more personally appropriate expectations and benchmarks.

In the years to come, there were decisions that I reached that were risky in my father's eyes, because they would jeopardize one of his paramount values—my security. In one case, I chose to put off applying to law school in order to start my tennis business. I felt that I had a great idea that no one had yet tried, and I knew that timing meant everything in this instance. My father's fear was that I'd get so wrapped up in some local tennis-instruction business that I'd never go back to school.

I thought things out, using my own value system as a base. Ultimately, my heart told me to start the business and, to my loving father's dismay, I did.

It was a huge success and an invaluable learning experience about real-life business and interpersonal dynamics. It helped me understand why business schools strongly prefer that their applicants have at least two years of business experience before enrollment. Within one year, the individuals in my company were teaching hundreds of students a week in specially designed group formats that I had devised. I also created and implemented all of the marketing and financial plans.

I then entered Cornell Law School (and business school) within fourteen months of starting the tennis clinic. Dad was relieved.

My business continued to run while I attended school. In this instance, I took Gardner Malloy's earlier advice and *Strategy* of having my cake and (later) eating it, too. This was to postpone school for a while in order to take advantage of a time-sensitive opportunity. Eventually, I pursued both—at their right and appropriate times. Also, in this case, Gardner's advice of *"It's the things that you never do that you'll always regret,"* rang more true for me.

In another example, several years later, I didn't accept any of the offers from law firms that I received upon graduation. My *Heart-of-Hearts* told me that I wouldn't be happy practicing corporate law. As I discussed earlier, there was a law position that I would have taken at an entertainment/sports law firm. However, the night before the hiring partner was to offer me the job, the individual who was supposed to leave the firm suddenly changed his mind. As a result, no offer was extended.

Instead, I decided to use some of the money that I had earned through my business to travel around the country and play tennis tournaments one last time (my *Rocky* fantasy). My other goal was to search my soul and try to come up with a profession, or at least a game plan, that would make me happy and make effective use of my talents.

When I told my dad that I had decided not to immediately take the bar exam and practice law but instead travel around the country, play tennis, and think, he perceived that his biggest fear for me was going to be realized: I would become a "tennis bum."

It was during this year off that I met the president of the William Morris Agency, at that time the world's most successful and prestigious theatrical agency. We had dinner, and I knew that I had found my calling.

I immediately began studying for the bar exam, and luckily, I passed it the first time around. I began working for William Morris, and loved every minute of it.

Interestingly, during the week that I started working for William Morris, the entertainment/sports law firm that had declined to make me the offer called to tell me that a spot had opened with them, and they could now offer me a position. The firm's offer was exactly twice the amount of money that I was making at William Morris—which was paying me peanuts. It took me about one minute to decide to stay.

Happiness took precedence. Besides, if I was good at what I did and loved it, I believed that enough money would eventually come.

When I turned down the law firm offer, the firm members felt that it was for monetary reasons, so they offered even more money. (These things always happen when you're either not looking for them or you no longer want them.) Once again, I passed on the offer, and explained to them that money wasn't the issue. I was really happy at William Morris, and I wasn't budging. But thanks.

Dad was at peace again.

Things stayed blissful for about five years. I was then transferred from the New York to the Los Angeles William Morris office. Eventually, Sam Weisbord, the president of William Morris, passed away. My overall mentor and role model, Lee Stevens, succeeded him. Unfortunately, soon after his promotion, Lee became ill and later died of a brain tumor.

As time went on, I realized that the individuals then running William Morris and I didn't share the same values—and that I couldn't live with theirs. At that time, I was vice president in charge of broadcasting for their West Coast office. I was well compensated by William Morris standards, and was certainly financially comfortable. But I wasn't happy. My heart told me that I had to leave. I flew home to tell my mom and dad. I knew that my dad wouldn't be happy.

I was enormously surprised. Maybe my dad had become desensitized, but he said, "Kenny, you've gone way beyond anything we could have dreamed for you. You've made us unbelievably proud of you. I just hope you know what you're doing. But it's your life. We're always here for you and we're always behind you, no matter what. We love you."

I promptly resigned from my position at William Morris.

Fifteen years later, my staff of fourteen and I have one of the most successful broadcasting agencies in the country. I am completely happy, professionally. I have the incredible opportunity to work with wonderfully talented individuals—our clients and my staff—as we all grow together. I also get to combine my love of people and being an entrepreneur with my legal and business backgrounds.

I'm happy, because I decided to follow my *Heart-of-Hearts*—and it hasn't let me down yet.

Strata-Gems:

- If you understand where a person is coming from, and you make a decision consistent with that information, you will be much more likely to have a positive result and experience.

- When making decisions, there are times that it's wise to listen and follow the subjective perspectives and advice of others. However, there are also times when you must follow your gut, your *Heart-of-Hearts*, and your own instincts, no matter what others may think or say.

- Don't let others' expectations shackle your decision-making. In the context of the *Big Picture*, feel psychologically and emotionally free to make the most self-enhancing decision possible.

UNDERSTANDING DEFENSES

When trying to make the wisest decisions possible, it is important to identify and understand the defensive thought processes, strategies, and behaviors of others, as well as your own.

Through my years of counseling, I've learned that defensive behavior, or "defense mechanisms," are behaviors that are adopted by individuals who, for a variety of reasons, feel especially vulnerable in some area(s) of their lives. As a means of coping, these individuals use their defense mechanisms to serve many purposes. In some instances, these mechanisms are used to conceal various feelings, insecurities, and vulnerabilities from the outside world ("external defenses"). In other instances, these defenses serve to protect and shield these vulnerable individuals from experiencing certain dissonant, conflicting inner feelings, and painful, unwanted stimuli ("internal defenses.") These defense mechanisms serve as effective disguises. Thus, what's real or true isn't always obvious, and your decision-making can be severely flawed if you rely on these disguises and false signals. As a result, it's crucial to see through these defenses and identify the truth.

Currently, we live in a world that generally doesn't go beyond the surface stimuli that are presented to us. Image over substance seems most often to be the norm. We have become so absorbed and isolated in our own protective bubbles that we rarely care enough to venture out to explore what others around us are really about. And when we're not so absorbed, we are often so uncertain or down about ourselves that we can't fathom that anyone else's lot in life can be as bad as ours, or that anyone can feel as angry or as lost as we do. So we tend to believe the rosy pictures others paint about themselves.

Additionally, in most instances, our society is ends- and not means-oriented—often, all that people respond to are the crafted signs of success that are purposely manufactured and sent out to us. We don't seem to question or to care whether these individuals actually have the "inner" goods to back them up. We want things quick and easy so that we can move on. Ours is fast becoming a society of contrived and manipulated personal and professional sales tools and images. Those of us using these tools and projecting these images, figure: "People will 'buy' my pitch, if I market it correctly."

In view of the above, let's change our vantage point and study defense mechanisms from the air and try to see the *Big Picture*. What about the person with the big ego, or the one who constantly brags while putting others down? If these individuals truly believed that it is evident to everyone how great they are, they wouldn't have to sell their qualities so hard and/or diminish others so much. In all likelihood, their apparent overconfidence is directly proportionate to how little self-worth and self-regard they really have. For example, when a client of mine sat next to an anchor who projected that he was God's gift to the world, the client said, "Boy, he really loves himself." I responded by telling her that nothing could be further from the truth. When you're confident and you know that you're good, you don't have to ram it down everyone's throat.

Some time ago, I slipped on the paddle tennis court and broke my elbow. Within minutes, the elbow had swelled up to the size of a softball. During my visit to the doctor, he explained to me that fluid gathers and surrounds the tender area to protect it from further bruising and damage.

It suddenly hit me. The swelling around my elbow is analogous to a big ego, or some other contrived communication, aimed at protecting and defending against the further bruising and damage to an already fragile and/or damaged self-image. In the case of the braggart, he or she has decided that the best defense is a strong outward display of offense; that is, a big show of confidence and invulnerability. The hoped-for effect is that the recipient of these signals will conclude that "This guy or gal sure is confident. They have it all going for them. He or she *must* know what they're doing." Not true! In this instance, it's all a smoke screen and a diversion from what's *really* going on inside.

Understanding Some "External" Differences

Through experience and observation, I've learned and counseled that people who are hostile and belligerent often have developed their "offensive" posture as a form of defense. These individuals lash out to keep people from further hurting them, possibly discovering and uncovering their vulnerability, and/or from seeing how hurt and rejected they truly feel. Time and again, their defensive behavior is used as a buffer to protect the raw feelings hidden within. In essence, these individuals appear to believe that: "If I attack you first, I might scare you off, and you won't get to me. Thus, I'm safe for the moment from hurt, disappointment, rejection, etc. Safe from people seeing the truth."

Another defensive strategy that I deal with on a regular basis is that of withdrawal or apathy. In these cases, individuals appear to withdraw from life and/or appear not to care, in order to conceal their low self-esteem and their intense fear of feeling more rejection and pain. These individuals, in some respects, take the opposite approach in order to protect themselves. They get out of the game altogether. If they don't get up to bat in the game of life, they can't strike out. If they don't put themselves into the contest, they can't be judged—and be rejected. These individuals appear as if—or say—they don't care. But deep down, they care, and once cared—big time. But as a result of past experiences of perceived or real rejection, they've chosen to never let themselves, or their expectations be rejected or dashed again. By withdrawing from it all, they're better safe than sorry.

Adopting the posture of being overly pleasing and obsequious is another way to protect ourselves. In this instance, people become chameleon-like, altering their behavior, opinions, and values in order to seek the love and approval of others. This behavior may be the result of these individuals feeling or perceiving that they were rejected or neglected by significant others when they were young. Therefore, in order to be valued by someone—or anyone—they attempt to curry the favor of others at all costs, including the loss of their dignity. This behavior is a defensive cover-up for how very little self-esteem and self-regard they have. At the root of this desperate need to constantly modify their behavior and compromise their true selves lies the profound inner perception that they will not be accepted for who they truly are, and that they aren't worthy of approval, value, and love. Therefore, they don't expose their true selves and they become actors, so to speak.

Each of the above defenses may be used individually or in combination with others. For example, when individuals act obsequiously, or don't express their true selves, they repress or suppress their true behaviors, opinions, and inclinations. As the repressed emotions increase and are pressed further and further down into the subconscious, one day, like a volcano, they may well explode into other behaviors,* including anger, hostility, and rage, directed at themselves and/or others. These behaviors can also be expressed as anger turned inward, such as the self-sabotaging acts of attempting or committing suicide, using recreational drugs, smoking cigarettes, or drinking excessive alcohol. In all of these cases, the individuals hurt themselves and subconsciously often want to hurt others. If individuals withdraw at first, once again, the bottled-up hurt and anger could eventually explode into the destructive behaviors outlined above.

In some instances, through various fortunate occurrences—planned or otherwise—some individuals take out their suppressed negativity by "sublimating" it. This occurs when they perform constructive acts such as athletics, acting, painting, etc., while at the same time nondestructively releasing their negative energy and pent-up anger or frustration. At times, I have done this with my tennis and paddle tennis. All of these activities can have a cathartic effect, and may help one learn and

*This concept of feeling or energy "transformation" is discussed in the next section.

adopt worthy values, as well as help gain approval from others. However, sublimation does not in any way guarantee these individuals the unconditional love and emotional support that they truly seek, although, they are more likely to be accepted and treated better when they decide to perform constructive rather than destructive acts.

Internal Defenses

In the above-mentioned instances, external defense mechanisms were adopted by individuals to use directly or indirectly with others. There are also *internal* defenses that we use to protect ourselves against experiencing internal conflict and pain. Some of these defenses are "rationalizations." They are cerebral ways to negotiate away and/or bury the internal conflict and pain, regarding a course of action that we plan to take, or have already engaged in. For example, Leon Festinger is credited with developing the theory of "cognitive dissonance." He says that when there is dissonance or conflict within, we often falsely modify our perception of one or more elements of the conflict, thereby bringing about a change that will help us negotiate and bring about consonance and harmony within. The conflict is thereby temporarily resolved and/or (speciously) eliminated.

For example, let's say a group of people stand in line for hours in the rain to get outrageously expensive New Year's Eve concert tickets. They eagerly await a long, excellent performance. However, instead of playing for an hour and a half, as they had every other night, the band played only for thirty minutes. To add insult to injury, they gave a lackluster and halfhearted performance. According to all reports, this was in apparent sharp contrast to the quality of their preceding six performances. At the end of the concert, the people who had stood in line for tickets for hours in the rain seethed inside. They knew that it had been a lousy experience compared with the experiences enjoyed by others on prior nights, and they also knew that there was nothing they could do about it. But as time went on, some of them wanted to find a way to feel better about the concert experience. So they began to rationalize that "The concert wasn't all that bad; in fact, it was pretty darn good"; that "Thirty minutes just hit the spot!"; and that "Because of all the crazies out on New Year's Eve and the torrential rain, it was better to get home early, anyway." These individuals thus manipulated their true perceptions in order to reach internal harmony. People often use rationalizations as Band-Aids to cover up their true feelings. The question in these cases is: When will the truth rise up and come to the fore in the form of anger, rage, or depression?

Another example: Your grandmother suddenly passes away, and you failed to visit her during the eight months preceding her death. You feel incredible guilt and sadness for being so self-absorbed that you didn't make time to see her. However, you rationalize that you *did* take her on an out-of-town trip two years ago, and during that trip, you spent quality time with her and told her that you loved her. So, you continue to rationalize, she knows how much she meant to you. You now feel somewhat better about not being with your grand-mother before her death. In this instance, rationalizing helps you to live with the mistake of not making time to see your beloved grand-mother before her passing.

However, when it comes to constructive and efficacious decision-making, the use of rationalizations can be poisonous. As we'll discuss below, you must see, identify, and deal with the unvarnished, uncom-promised truth when reaching your decisions, or else they may well be flawed.

Here are some illustrations of how individuals have used rational-izations in order to justify their problematic behavior:

- Joe implies to his friends that he was having an extramarital affair, unbeknownst to his new spouse. When someone in-quires, "Don't you feel bad about cheating on Sue?" Joe quickly replies—as though this was not the first time that this question had been thrown at him—"Well, yeah, sometimes. But listen, there are no angels, right?"

- When some high school boys are asked whether it is "cool" to take recreational drugs, drink excessively, harass or sexually molest female class members, they respond that others in their class are doing it and getting away with it, so it must be OK.

• When individuals who sell drugs and cigarettes to kids are asked how they can "live with" doing something so harmful, some reply, "I have to. I need to feed myself and my family, don't I?"

• When an attorney is asked how he could live with himself after successfully defending a repeat rapist he knows is guilty, he responds, "Why not? It's the justice system. Everyone's entitled to the best defense. If I don't do it, somebody else will get the $100,000 legal fee. It might as well be me."

• An executive in a company often treats his longtime, efficient, and hard-working assistant without respect, displaces his anger onto her, and publicly humiliates her. When associates call him on these ugly actions, he explains, "There shouldn't be a problem with my behavior; that's how I was treated by my boss. And besides, every Christmas I give her a big box of candy and fruit for her and her family. I make it up to her."

These examples all illustrate various excuses and bootstrap arguments that are used to reach flawed and dangerous conclusions. And it is these conclusions that seemingly allow us to decide to act in destructive ways and to avoid dealing with the unattractive truth. Instead of identifying and trying to rectify the real internal problem with exploratory surgery, we spray the concern with Bactine—that is, we rationalize it—in an effort to disinfect the site and making it feel good for the moment.

By deciding to use internal "spin" mechanisms (strategies) such as rationalizations, repressing true feelings, and attempting to lie to oneself and to others, you can become completely alienated from who you truly are and the kind of person who you truly aspire to be. Maybe this is why many of us feel so lost and empty, so compromised.

Additionally, as people rationalize that destructive actions and strategies such as violence, substance abuse, inhumanity to others, etc., are okay, we all sink and become morally and spiritually desensitized and diminished. We risk forgetting or losing touch with what's right and humane. And as we will discuss later, acting poorly lowers our feelings of self-esteem and self-worth. As a result, we are much more likely to continue to make destructive and self-sabotaging decisions in the future.

At this juncture, I'd like to share a story about John, who regularly used external and internal defenses to his great detriment.

John is an advertising executive for a high-powered ad firm. In many ways, both personally and professionally, he's got great energy and can be wonderful to be around. He also has a good and warm heart. However, John is much more street smart than book smart, and he can be very insecure about his intellect. He often compensates for his perceived inadequacies quite well by working his butt off. He's the most aggressive and relentless person imaginable when seeking out new clients for his company. The problem is, John is one of the most defensive individuals walking the planet. As his friend, this concerns me a great deal, and it's also quite irritating.

At dinner one night, he vented for hours about a heated conversation that he had earlier in the day with his boss, Todd, who is friends with both of us. Apparently Todd and the other partners of his firm wanted to grow and expand John's department. They were hoping that some of the many assistants that John had trained through the years would move up the ladder and become ad execs, just as John was allowed and encouraged to do. The issue that Todd termed "serious and out of control" was the fact that, out of the twenty assistants that John had trained during the seven years that he had been with the company, none—*not one*—had stayed around to be promoted.

John had a couple of them fired. But mostly, they all left, saying that John was so territorial about his work and his clients that they couldn't learn anything and therefore couldn't and wouldn't grow. Three assistants left with ulcers; one alleged a nervous disorder. They all felt that John was a good person who wanted his assistants to be just that—his assistants. He didn't want anyone growing or competing with him in any way.

Todd explained to John how exasperating and inefficient it was to expend great amounts of time and money training all of these individuals, only to have them quit and go to work—many of them successfully—for other firms, because John was too insecure to let them assume any responsibility. Apparently, John then spent the next hour or so explaining either why each and every one of his former twenty assistants wasn't worthy of growth in the firm, or why he wasn't in any way at fault for their departures. According to Todd, John didn't spend one minute of the seemingly endless meeting even considering the possible role that his own behavior or thought processes had played.

Finally, when Todd had reached the end of his rope, he sarcastically asked, "John, are you telling me that all the assistants you've had, who have *all* complained at one time or another that you won't let them in and won't let them grow, are making this stuff up?"

John offensively shot back, "Yes," and proceeded to explain, ad nauseam, why none of them was "right" or deserved to be promoted. He then assured Todd that when an assistant who *was* worthy of a promotion did come along, he would be more than happy to see them promoted.

Knowing how insecure John was, Todd didn't believe that one for a second. Todd then discussed with John the fact that he had been losing a great many clients recently, to which John quickly replied that he had also been bringing in a great number of clients over the past year, as well.

Todd, trying to keep John focused on the issue at hand, continued by asking him why he thought that all the clients were leaving him? He answered by blaming everyone and everything around him—including the clients' "lack of character." He never assumed any responsibility for, or questioned his role in, the defections.

Todd finally blurted out, "John, you are the most defensive person I've ever met. You live in your own little world and have your own reality. When there is a problem, it's *never* caused by anything you've done. You're perfect, right? Can't you see that you're sabotaging your assistants, and how damaging this is to the firm?"

When attacked, John could be counted on to respond in his usual aggressive, self-righteous manner. And counterattack he did, raising both his voice and his intensity level: "Todd, I work harder than *anyone* in this firm. I've given my life to you and your partners. Is this what I get to show for it?

Todd ended the meeting by telling John that he should take some time and think about what they had discussed at their meeting, and that they would speak again soon.

After hearing John's version of the meeting, and having already gotten a call from Todd in which he explained his perspective, I asked John if he felt that he might in any way be at fault for the departures of the assistants or the clients. He spent the next half hour or so explaining to me—as if it were as clear as it could be—how right he was, and how *others* had caused all the problems.

Todd was correct. John just didn't get it. And didn't want to.

A week or two later, when there was no real change in John's perspective regarding the issues raised at the meeting, Todd, with great sadness, had to inform John that the firm's board of directors had decided that it probably would be best if John quietly looked around for a position at another firm, because in all likelihood, he wouldn't grow any further with them.

When John was able to get beyond his shock, he combatively added, "So, this is over the assistants, huh?" Todd quietly confided, "No, John. Not really. It's about the fact that because you're so defensive, you can't see the truth; and if you can't see the truth, you'll never grow and you'll stop us from growing. Unfortunately, the board feels that, being as you are, you're incapable of changing. *That's* why. But as your friend, I do hope you learn from this."

As Todd left the room, John yelled at the top of his lungs, "Todd, this is how you repay me for all I've done! You're gonna be sorry you ever let me walk away! *Really* sorry!"

Unfortunately, I've seen too many individuals—wonderful and

talented ones—rationalize away self-destructive or bad behavior. They revise history in their minds and spin or distort the truth so that they can feel OK about doing negative and hurtful things to themselves and to others.

If you're to become a constructive decision-maker and an active and compassionate *Student of Life*, you must continually seek out and assimilate the best data available, test it against what you already know, and, depending on the results, either continue to think and act the same way, or modify your thoughts, decisions, and actions in accordance with the new and better information that you've culled from your analysis. This way, you're always learning and/or growing. A key factor in your success in this endeavor is that you must base your decisions on *honesty, objectivity, and what's true*—not on rationalizations, or what you'd like to be true, or what you'd be most comfortable believing is true.

If you're not honest with yourself and don't deal with what's true or factual—as John apparently wasn't and didn't—your thinking, perceptions, and decisions will be highly flawed, and you won't grow. The fact is, *you will be sabotaging yourself more than any person could ever sabotage you*.

So be open and honest enough to recognize and accept your mistakes, your shortcomings, and what's *real*. Only then can you improve.

In the process of making decisions involving other individuals, you must always be cognizant of the fact that outward appearances may not be an accurate indication of what these individuals truly think or feel. When you are trying to interpret someone's behavior, step away in an attempt to discern whether the strategies of external defenses and rationalizations are involved, and if they are, what they are designed to accomplish and protect. Being aware of and exploring these questions will help you to better understand others and/or a given situation, and provide you with a more accurate indication as to how you can choose to feel and/or act in a given circumstance.

Additionally, when trying to make the wisest decisions, you must deal with the truth about yourself—the truth about how you really feel, what you really value, and what you really aspire to achieve. Rationalizations cover up the truth, and if they're not identified, and your true feelings aren't explored, you very likely will reach flawed, weak, and counterproductive decisions.

Strata-Gem:

It is crucial to see through your defenses and rationalizations— and those of others—in order for you to craft your most effective, realistic, and enhancing decisions.

CORRECTING AND ENHANCING
VERSUS OVERCOMPENSATING

The two most important problem-solving *Strategies* that I learned while in law school are: When faced with a problem, first try to understand the situation, and second, identify the crux of the problem, or, as we used to say, "spot the (real) issue." (For example, one must identify whether the case at hand is one of negligence, breach of contract, etc.) By performing these two steps, we are then better able to decide upon the best course of action, resolution, or proactive, enhancing solution to the problem.

One *Strategy* that runs throughout *Crunch Time*, is that you must constantly strive to gather and assimilate data, and if and when you find that your *Strategies* aren't producing the enhancing results that you desire, you must correct and adjust—in essence, rework—those *Strategies*. This process is objective, constructive, and proactive. There is an openness about it, in that you must be open to admitting, "I'm not perfect and neither are my *Strategies*, but I'm open to understanding what my deficiencies are, and open to exploring what the crux of the problems are, so that I can go on to modify my *Strategies* or adopt new ones, and thus enhance and improve my life."

This corrective *Strategy* is in direct contrast to the often destructive strategy of overcompensation, which is aimed at subjectively, defensively, and reactively covering up for one's perceived deficiencies.

The *Strategy* of overcompensation is one of the most prevalent, self-defeating—rather than self-enhancing—behavioral patterns that

I have come across. To illustrate the dynamics of this *Strategy,* let me depict three scenarios that, for the most part, raise similar issues.

A local-station morning-show host, who had been a serious network news correspondent prior to assuming his hosting duties, had the following experience and reaction. One day, after he finished his show and was walking back to his office, he ran into a news anchor at his station, who sarcastically chided him, "So how are those cooking segments going?"

The host became quite upset and defensive at hearing the remark. He perceived that the intended implication was that he had forsaken his journalistic ideals. The host's on-air performance changed immediately thereafter. From that point on, his demeanor on the previously light and fun morning show became serious and sullen, and he became confrontational with his guests. The morning-show host had already established, during his network news correspondent days, that he was a very good journalist. Evidently, he didn't really believe it, as he allowed himself to feel put down and diminished by someone who wasn't important in the grand scheme of things.

For this and other reasons, viewership for the show slipped, and he became more of a liability than an asset. Eventually, he was replaced as host of the show and his contract wasn't renewed.

In another scenario, a beautiful female with a wonderfully warm, effervescent and engaging presence was offered the extraordinary opportunity to become a host on a nationally syndicated entertainment program. At the time, she was making a transition from being a fashion model and commercial actress to becoming a TV broadcaster. Because some detractors commented that she was "all looks and no substance," she was determined to be taken seriously and to be viewed as intelligent. As a result, she chose to decline the extremely attractive national offer. Instead, she decided to find a hard-news anchor position in a local market. After many months of being out of work and looking, she finally secured an anchor job in a small market earning about twenty percent of what she would have been paid as the host of the national entertainment show). In trying to fulfill her quest to be taken seriously, she was so cold, stern, and icy on the air that she turned off the viewers . . . as well as the management of her station. She lasted about nine months before she and her station had a mutual parting of ways.

In the final scenario, a top-ranked tennis player, who had won numerous major championships early in his career, allegedly became angered by the comment made about him that he couldn't win without being totally dependent on his explosive and extremely effective serve and volley game. As a response, the player changed his tactics and began to rely much less on his lethal serves and volleys. Instead, he began to hit many more ground strokes. To his dismay, he has never again been as successful as he was before he changed his game plan.

In the three scenarios outlined above, all three individuals reacted by defensively overcompensating for a felt inadequacy that they harbored within. They also proceeded to go down the tubes as a result of their destructive decisions and *Strategies*.

If these individuals had their decisions to make over again, and they truly aspired to be constructive *Crunch Time* performers, they could step back from the situation they were involved in and examine their behavior from the perspective of the *Big Picture*. This could help them answer a number of all-important questions:

1a) Why did the morning-show host feel that he needed to constantly remind everyone of what a good journalist he was, despite the fact that his new behavior, in many instances, was inappropriate and job threatening?

1b) What did the host, in his *Heart-of-Hearts*, truly want to accomplish with his decision?

1c) What was the most self-enhancing way to correct and improve his situation? In essence, what would make it a win/win situation, or at least the most positive one possible?

2a) Why did the female choose not to take a national position that she was incredibly well-suited for, and then, in the job that she did take, perform in an inappropriate manner?

2b) What did the female, in her *Heart-of-Hearts*, truly want to accomplish with her decisions?

2c) What was the most self-enhancing way to take advantage of the national entertainment program host offer, so as to make it a win/win situation for her?

3a) Why did the tennis player choose to show everyone how well-rounded his tennis game was, at great risk and cost to his success and career?

3b) What did the tennis player, in his *Heart-of-Hearts*, truly want to accomplish with his decision?

3c) What was the most self-enhancing means to correct and improve his *Strategy*, so as to help him achieve all of his goals?

In the instances described above, all three individuals felt criticized and somehow diminished. In a sense, they then developed "tunnel vision," focusing only on their feelings of hurt, anger, and apparent inadequacy. They each reacted with the sole purpose of counteracting the felt criticism, to the exclusion of all other valid factors and possibilities in the situation. To the degree that this was the case, they severely limited the scope of their objectivity in a very concrete way, and limited the possibility of considering and pursuing alternate options and strategies. Without a doubt, up until the point when they experienced the criticism, their situations, for all practical purposes, appeared to be quite positive. In actuality, nothing had really changed in their situations except for their own feelings—which then turned negative—based solely on incidental criticism that was of no real consequence.

In all three of the instances outlined above, the individuals needed to proactively and objectively explore what alternative behavioral strategies might have been more constructive ways to achieve their true, unadulterated (by hurt and anger) heartfelt values and desires. For example, the morning host could have requested that he do some hard-news-reporting assignments along with his light hosting duties. If this could have been accomplished, he could have then derived the pleasure and satisfaction of being a journalist again, and he could have also shown his detractors that he is a well-balanced newsperson, because he hosts and also reports. This situation might well have provided a means for the host to feel more comfortable about having fun and being warm on the morning show, which required a light, soft touch for ratings success.

Similarly, the female could have accepted the national host position and then requested that she cover some of the current harder-edged entertainment stories, such as the O.J. and Marv Albert trials, along with other more serious stories. Local stations that aired her entertainment program might well have welcomed the opportunity to have her do some in-depth stories of her choosing, just to have a national host on their station. Additionally, there might have been venues, such as cable television, where she could have done some in-depth interviews that would have showcased her intelligence and her interviewing and writing skills. The constructive decision, in this instance, would have been for her to take and then make the most of the high-profile national host position, by seeking out and finding appropriate avenues to fulfill her hard-news goals while allowing others (her own show, local stations, cable networks, etc.), to reap the benefit of having her appear on their programs. This would have been a win/win/win decision to make and act out.

In the case of the tennis player, instead of essentially abandoning his successful dominating serve and volley game for the sake of hitting almost all ground strokes, he could have changed his *Strategy* to one that allowed him to use *all* of his weapons at the appropriate times. This way, instead of falling from the top of the tennis rankings, he might have improved his already strong game and gone on to achieve even greater accomplishments.

In the above scenarios, all three individuals reacted so defensively—by deciding to adopt the destructive (subjective) *Strategy* and behavior of overcompensation—that they never gave themselves the opportunity to objectively explore what their real problems were and what constructive, self-enhancing alternative options and/or solutions could have been created.

These individuals also needed to explore, analyze, and determine, as objectively as possible, the real agendas of those who made the derogatory and/or disrespectful comments to and about them. In addition, they needed to explore their own reactions to the comments openly, in order to discern why they felt the urge to react so strongly, defensively, and rashly. Only then could they begin to determine, in any balanced way, what an appropriate response to those detractors might have been—or if any response, in the *Big Picture*, would have been appropriate at all. Had these three individuals followed some of our *Crunch Time Strategies* or *Strata-Gems*, they might have come to see that the real issue was not about what others said or did. Rather, it was how these three felt about themselves and how they destructively attempted to cover up their perceived flaws and insecurities.

Strata-Gem:

When you are faced with perceived problems, flaws and weaknesses, don't react by deciding to adopt the defensive and diminishing strategies of tunnel vision and overcompensation. Instead, be open to objectively and proactively analyzing and assessing your current situation and your past *Strategies* and behaviors, and when it is appropriate, correct and improve them, or craft completely new, creative, and enhancing ones.

APPLYING THE
CRUNCH TIME STRATEGIES

Now that we have discussed the *Crunch Time Strategies*, let's go back to *Step 3* and explore and decide which of these *Strategies*, and which of the *Strategies* that you've created, will most effectively help you to reach an enhancing, success-evoking decision, given the issue at hand.

As an illustration of *Step 3*, let's go back to my client, Julianna, who was faced with the issue of whether she would forgo her much-awaited and extensively planned vacation with her husband so that she could fill in for the individual whose anchor position she desired to succeed to.

Once Julianna identified that a decision needed to be made and she clearly stated to herself what the issue was, she applied the following *Strategies* to help her make a decision that we both believe ultimately led to her securing the anchor position that she coveted.

1) First, when Julianna's news director asked her to postpone her vacation just five days before her scheduled departure, she listened, but didn't react. She delayed her response until she could thoroughly and objectively explore her options. (*Strategy #1: Think, and then choose your actions; don't react.*) When she did respond, she was wise to carefully explain her predicament to him, but she also said that she wanted

to be a team player, and that she would do everything possible to try to help him and the station.

This was truly constructive *Crunch Time* thinking and decision-making. Julianna chose her responses carefully and effectively. Through well-thought-out communication, she made sure that her news manager was aware of all of the plans—both hers and her husband's—that had been made regarding the vacation, so in case she couldn't or wouldn't change her vacation, he might better understand why. And if she did rearrange her trip, he would hopefully better appreciate all that she had done. (*Strategy #2: Communicate effectively, so that it touches the listener.*)

She consciously expressed her sentiments about wanting to be a team player, and that she would do everything she could to try and work things out, because she knew, that in the past, other anchors had not been team players, and that the news manager had resented it. (*Strategy #3: Understand where others are coming from.*) As I mentioned earlier, I often recommend the *Strategy* of, "You get more flies with honey than with vinegar." In this case, despite the fact that my client felt that a great deal of pressure was being exerted on her to postpone her vacation, she didn't act negatively. Instead, she used a warm, constructive response that she knew her news manager would respect and respond to positively. By doing this, she seized the opportunity to bring him philosophically closer to her. (*Strategy #4: Know who your audience is, and find an effective means to connect with them.*)

Finally, she told her manager that she would need some time to see what she could do about rearranging her vacation. This period of time would give her the opportunity to carefully think things through, with the aim that she would ultimately make her very best decision under the circumstances. (*Strategy #5: Take the requisite time to reach your best decision.*)

2) The next thing that Julianna did was to step away from the situation, first by herself and then with me. She looked at and considered her options in the context of the *Big Picture* of her broadcasting career (*Strategy #6: View your decision in the context of the Big Picture of your*

life and the attainment of your most cherished goals and dreams), her relationship with her husband and what his wants and needs were, and the state of her overall mental and physical health. (*Strategy #7: Explore the appropriate values*). Upon viewing the *Big Picture*, she assessed that doing all that she could to secure the top anchor position—at an excellent station, in a city that she desired to make her long-term home—was a top priority and value. (*Strategy #8: Identify a top-priority value.*) And although she was both disappointed that she couldn't take her vacation and irked that the news manager had waited until the last minute to make his request, she determined that she was not so mentally or physically tired that her health was at risk if she were to delay her vacation for a month or so. (*Strategy #9: Discern how you, in your Heart-of-Hearts, truly feel.*) Additionally, after consulting with her understanding and supportive husband, she learned that he would be OK with postponing their time off. He loved his wife, encouraged her professionally, and knew and appreciated the great value that getting the weeknight anchor position had for her. (*Strategy #10: Learn and accurately understand the feelings and values of relevant others.*)

3) After jointly and objectively examining the *Big Picture*, Julianna (and her husband) realized that this was an occasion to delay the gratification of taking their vacation—for the time being—in the hope of getting a bigger payoff later. (*Strategy #11: Delay gratification.*)

4) Julianna also objectively and correctly assessed her competition (Cindy) for the weeknight anchor position. She acknowledged that Cindy was in fact talented, and if she were given the opportunity to fill in for the two weeks, she might well become a much more serious threat to get the weeknight job when it became available. (*Strategy #12: Accurately assess relevant others' agendas and strengths; and Strategy #13: When possible, don't allow a variable to enter into a situation—such as Cindy filling in—over which you have no control.*)

5) Julianna also took time to assess the various agendas of the individuals who were involved in her decision. Although she knew that her

husband was looking forward to their vacation, and that he had taken pains to clear the time from his own very demanding professional schedule, she also knew that he truly appreciated what was at stake for her, and that he would be supportive if the vacation were postponed. Julianna also sensed that her news manager was behind her, and that if he wanted her to postpone her vacation and fill in, he must have had a good reason. She also knew that Cindy wanted nothing more than to fill in for the two weeks and to leap-frog over Julianna and get the weeknight job. (*Strategy #14: More assessment of relevant others' motives and agendas.*)

6) Julianna knew that she had gotten off to a good start at the station by immediately being pegged as the number-two anchor there. By temporarily forgoing her vacation and not giving Cindy the opportunity to fill in, she would in all likelihood maintain that position. This would greatly increase her chances of becoming the number-one female anchor when the opportunity arose. (*Strategy #15: Put the percentages in your favor to secure a successful outcome.*)

7) Julianna realized that in order to attain her dreams, she would from time to time have to be flexible and adopt a soft-hands approach. (*Strategy #16: Be flexible and adaptable.*) In this instance, she was disappointed and a bit angry that her plans had to be quickly changed, but she also knew that she needed to have a positive—or at least an accepting—mind-set if she indeed did change her plans. She didn't want any of her feelings of disappointment or anger to show on the air, because if they were evident, then rearranging her vacation to fill in would turn out to be counterproductive. In essence, if she performed poorly, she could set herself back. (*Strategy #17: Use appropriate discipline.*) We both agreed with the *Strategy* of: "If you're going to do something good (e.g., sacrifice your vacation), the intended recipients (in this case, Julianna's news management and her audience) need to enjoy it, otherwise, the well-conceived effort can mean nothing, or can even work against you." (*Strategy #18: Act constructively.*)

8) Julianna recognized that winning the battle of being able to take her vacation as scheduled—because she was able to get her news manager to understand her predicament—would be no victory at all if she lost the war and Cindy did such a good job of filling in that Cindy was given the weeknight position instead. (*Strategy #19: Honestly and non-defensively assess the situation, and then identify the issue before you.*)

9) Julianna continued to look at the issues through the grander perspective of the *Big Picture* in order to see if there were any alternative ways of approaching the situation that she hadn't yet thought of and/or explored. (*Strategy #20: Explore your decision in the context of the Big Picture.*) She asked: "Was there any constructive way to take her vacation as planned and still keep herself in the best position possible to later get the main anchor job? Was there a win/win solution here?" We came up with one possible alternative. I would call her news manager and ask that his station consider not only committing to Julianna becoming the main weeknight anchor upon the incumbent's departure, but also negotiating a new, more lucrative agreement reflecting this promotion—*before* Julianna's vacation. (*Strategy #21: Be a creative strategist and decision-maker.*) The news manager responded that had the prior general manager still been running the station, our proposal might well have been accepted, but with a new general manager in place, he wasn't ready to make any commitments of that magnitude. He needed to watch Julianna a bit more before making any long-term decisions.

10) Julianna then applied one of the *Crunch Time Strategies* that she often used, and that had produced positive results for her in the past. Her *Strategy* of carpe diem was: "Like a fullback in football, when you see a hole (an opening), run like hell for the daylight, and keep running until you score (the touchdown)." In other words, if you have an opportunity to proactively seize your goal, do it. (*Strategy #22: When the right opportunity presents itself, seize it!*) Julianna was appropriately confident about her anchoring skills. Therefore, she felt strongly that if she filled in for the two weeks, she'd significantly enhance her chances to get the weeknight position permanently.

11) After applying the appropriate *Strategies*, as well as the remainder of the *Eight Steps*, Julianna decided to postpone her vacation. (= *Decision*)

12) We then engaged in some Pre–*Crunch Time, Out-of-the-Box* decision-making. She and I decided that along with Julianna telling the news manager that she would change her plans, I would also ask the station to reimburse any expenses that she and her husband incurred in changing their reservations, along with the station committing to two specific weeks of vacation, plus some other holidays off, for Julianna later that year. The news manager happily agreed to all of our requests. (*Strategy #23: When appropriate, use an Out-of-the-Box Strategy to effect a desirable outcome.*) I also reiterated to him that Julianna was truly a team player, and that I hoped that her team spirit would serve her well when the station managers were deciding who should become their next weeknight anchor. He said that her professionalism would serve her well.

After using the twenty-three different *Strategies* indicated above, Julianna made a decision that proved to be both wise and efficacious. Her talents and professionalism—along with her objective and constructive decision-making processes—did serve her well. Three weeks later she was selected as the new weeknight anchor of her station.

Once again, *Step 3* provides that you explore and then apply the appropriate *Crunch Time Strategies* and *Strata-Gems*, and any other constructive *Strategies* that you've created, to the issue before you.

PART
3

Completing the Process

Step 4

IDENTIFY, EXPLORE, AND WEIGH YOUR MOST IMPORTANT AND ENHANCING VALUES

In reaching self-enhancing decisions, you must know what result you truly desire to secure from your decision. In essence, you have to identify what you really want. As we discussed earlier, this often involves the honest, non-defensive *Heart-of-Hearts* exploration and weighing of various, sometimes conflicting, values. To illustrate these steps, let's briefly revisit some of the stories presented in prior chapters.

1) My client Julianna really wanted to take her long-awaited and much needed vacation with her equally excited husband. But when she weighed her competing values in the context of what she most wanted in the *Big Picture* of her life, she concluded that she wanted the weeknight anchor job at her station more.

2) As a child, I loved and craved fattening foods. However, when I honestly searched my *Heart-of-Hearts*, I found that I enjoyed being thinner, athletically successful, and physically attractive much, much more, than the momentary pleasure of eating food that put or kept excess weight on me.

3) In the Matt Lauer/*Today* show story, we learned that Matt identified a number of attractive values on both sides of

the equation that he had to weigh. Here is my perception of the most prominent ones:

Today	*Access Hollywood*
1) Matt's ultimate dream job.	1) It was a dream job, especially before Matt became a member of *Today*.
2) It satisfied his passion for interviewing interesting and diverse individuals in a "live" setting.	2) It would be a very positive career step to take, if hosting a national entertainment program was his true desire.
3) In a relatively up-and-down career, he was enjoying unprecedented positive response as both the *Today* newsreader and fill-in host.	3) NBC management encouraged him to accept the position; it's always nice to please your employer, especially if that employer has been good to you.
4) If he remained at *Today*, Matt was on track to host one of the network morning news programs.	4) NBC management told Matt that if the male host position on *Today* became available, he could come back and take it (if he were deemed the best candidate).
5) If he hosted *Access Hollywood*, he might never again be a viable candidate to host a network morning news show.	5) The salary for *Access* would be two or three times what he was currently earning.
	6) There was not a hint of evidence that if Matt opted not to accept the *Access* offer, and he remained as the newsreader on *Today*, Bryant Gumbel would leave his host position anytime in the foreseeable future.

As we know, after carefully identifying, exploring, and weighing the aforementioned values, Matt decided to stay at *Today*, and his great decision has paid off royally ever since.

Step 4 is for you to take as much time as is necessary and available to dig deep and sincerely and honestly search your *Heart-of-Hearts*, in order to identify, explore, and weigh your most cherished values and goals in the context of the decision that you will make.

Knowing what you truly want for yourself and what will make your heart sing in the *Big Picture* of your life is a major step in your reaching the most self-enhancing, constructive, wise, and appropriate short- and long-term decisions before, during, and after *Crunch Time*. It will also motivate and inspire you to stick with those decisions— even during crisis periods and moments of weakness. And as you may well have experienced, sticking with your constructive decisions over time often is the hardest thing to do. We will discuss how to success- fully meet this challenge in upcoming *Steps*.

Step 5

EXPLORE HOW YOUR
DECISION WILL
AFFECT YOUR
HEART-OF-HEARTS

THE THREE Cs OF HIGH SELF-ESTEEM
DECISION-MAKING: BE CONSTRUCTIVE,
SHOW CONSIDERATION FOR OTHERS,
HAVE CHARACTER

Step 5 involves an honest exploration as to how the decision that you're about to make will effect your *Heart-of-Hearts*. This step is crucial to your psychological and emotional happiness and well-being. So it makes sense at this juncture for us to study and understand the concept of our *Heart-of-Hearts*.

YOUR STRATEGIES AND BEHAVIOR
PATTERNS, AND YOUR *HEART-OF-HEARTS*

Throughout our journey together, I discuss both the importance of embracing and following constructive and enhancing *Strategies* for decision-making and behavior, as well as the dangers inherent in adopting self-diminishing and destructive decision-making *Strategies*. There's no question that it is the *Strategies* that you decide to make your own, and then act out, that can make all the difference in determining the quality of the life that you lead . . . and whether you develop feelings of high or low self-esteem and self-worth in the process.

Experience has taught me that by choosing and following the right *Strategies* (i.e., those that are the most self-and/or life-enhancing), you can seize your highest potentials and make them realities. This being so, it would greatly behoove you to rework and/or polish your *Strategies*, as well as to fashion new, constructive ones. In this regard, and to facilitate the process, it is exceedingly important to understand why and how we adopt our original life *Strategies* and where they come from.

It's arguable that all of us have a profound need to be loved and treasured, a need that we experience in the deepest recesses of our beings. This need, as I understand it, is two-pronged: Not only must we in fact be loved, treasured, and respected, but we must also *feel* loved, cherished, and respected by our parents, key caregivers, and significant others. Since children aren't mind readers, the love and treasuring given to them must be communicated in ways that children can personally recognize, understand, and experience from the moment of birth onward (i.e., initially through touch, sound, and warmth). So even if parents have the best of intentions, if they can't effectively communicate their love to their children (so that their children understand, experience and/or *feel* that love, it's all for naught). As time goes on, children will subjectively interpret the stimuli that they take in (i.e., how parents and significant others act toward them) as a means of determining how these individuals feel about them and ultimately, how these children should feel about themselves.

Looking at the *Big Picture* of my development, it's clear that it was how I felt and how I perceived that my needs were or weren't met in a given situation that determined both whether I had positive or negative feelings about certain things or individuals, and whether I made constructive or destructive decisions regarding them thereafter.

It's how children's needs are met and how children subjectively perceive and feel that they are regarded that has a major and lasting impact upon them, and ultimately, that determines what *Strategies* they will adopt and act out during the course of their lives. This concept can most easily be explained through imagination and visualization.

First, create and visualize in your mind a highly simplified metaphorical version of a child's heart. In the depths of this metaphorical heart is a magic place. (This is similar to the metaphorical and/or metaphysical concept of the "seat" of your soul, or the core of your being, and acts much like the mind as it functions and relates to the brain.) I refer to this metaphorical, magical place as the *Heart-of-Hearts*.

Except for a small, but strong metaphorical "magnet" within that represents the child's fundamental and primal needs, the *Heart-of-Hearts* appears relatively empty (unfilled) at birth. The primary function of this magnet is to attract and draw in emotional stimuli from the outer world.

These stimuli are then recognized and received either as nurturing and enhancing, or as diminishing and hurtful. Thus, the child's *Heart-of-Hearts* is gradually filled with whatever is experienced and drawn in from the child's outer world—from the very beginning of the child's life.

Now, think back and try to remember and visualize what it was like to be an innocent child, completely open and trusting, needing love, approval, and acceptance in order to flourish psychologically, while at the same time being just as completely open, trusting, vulnerable, and wholly defenseless against rejection, hurt, pain, disappointment, etc.—all at the hands of parents and/or the significant others you were exposed to and totally dependent upon during your childhood years. The subsequent impact of all of this on "you" (i.e., your psyche, your soul, your *Heart-of-Hearts*) was most profound. It touched and influenced the very core of your being—for better or worse—depending on how you perceived the experiences. In this regard, you must stay fully aware that because all children and adults are exposed to various stimuli, they each perceive and process them in their own subjective ways.

Next, imagine that the *Heart-of-Hearts* is magical, because it has the power, in certain instances, to process one form of energy into another—such as when the gases of hydrogen and oxygen are transformed into water, when water is boiled and transformed into steam, or when water is frozen and transformed into ice, etc.

When the *Heart-of-Hearts* draws in both the positive and negative stimuli that it receives from the outside world, it magically transforms them from sensory perceptions into various good and bad feelings that, in turn, fill it up. Thereafter, if the amount of felt love, positive valuing, and respect in the *Heart-of-Hearts* is plentiful enough to exceed a specific threshold (the complete filling of the *Heart-of-Hearts*), then there are enough feelings of love, self-esteem, and self-respect for some of the feelings to be transformed into other feelings: first, into self-love; then, into the love of others; and finally, into altruism.

Feelings of being loved → high self-esteem and self-respect → self-love → love of others → altruistic love

Optimally, a child's *Heart-of-Hearts* will be filled to overflowing with feelings of love and being cherished, which have been bestowed upon the child from the moment of birth by parents and/or other key caregivers. Once a child's *Heart-of-Hearts* is filled with love and other positive feelings, there will be no room left within the *Heart-of-Hearts* for any negative stimuli to penetrate. In essence, the child's *Heart-of-Hearts* is so well insulated and fortified psychologically, emotionally, and spiritually by positive feelings that the negativity rolls off the child like water rolls off a duck's back. Maybe this, in part, explains why some children and adults can be exposed to negative stimuli, such as violent films, TV programs, and music, without being affected by them, whereas others are catalyzed to commit destructive acts.

If a child's *Heart-of-Hearts* is left partially or totally unfilled with positive feelings from parents and significant others, this can allow the magnet within (the child's needs) to indiscriminately attract both negative and positive stimuli to fill the *Heart-of-Hearts*—and the big problem today is that there are so many negative stimuli in our society to attract (violence, crime, and poor role models, to name just a few).

In many instances, when feelings of being loved, valued, and respected aren't initially forthcoming from parents or significant others in a child's life, and when these positive feelings are perceived by the child to be totally unavailable, the *Heart-of-Hearts* frequently fills up and begins to overflow with overwhelming feelings of unlovability, unworthiness, rejection, betrayal, inadequacy, shame, hurt, resentment, alienation, insecurity, and powerlessness, depending upon what the child perceives and/or experiences.

Along with the feelings of unlovability and hurt, etc., there also develops a sense of extreme vulnerability and an intense fear of having that vulnerability exposed. At some point during this process, the child's hunger for love, valuing, approval, and respect is psychologically suppressed (i.e., as a defense mechanism, it is pressed back into the *Heart-of-Hearts*, where it is transformed). From then on, new needs arise: protection, power, control, and revenge. However, despite the fact that a large variety of rationalizations, as well as a number of other coping and defense mechanisms (*Strategies*), may have been developed and put into place when frustration after frustration, and hurt after hurt, are added to the already existing negative feelings, they are all too often transformed in the *Heart-of-Hearts* of a child or an adult into the unreasoning and powerful emotions of intense anger, rage, and hate.

Feeling unloved → frustration → pain and hurt → resentment, anger, and rage → destructiveness

When these emotions come into play, as they are forced to in almost all love-starved cases, they can and often do result in destructive actions taken by those experiencing them. These actions may be taken against oneself—like self-sabotage—and/or against others. Sometimes these actions aren't related to the behavior of the targeted person, such as in the instance of displaced anger, when, for example, a boss has a negative encounter with his wife, child, or valued client and then immediately thereafter yells at or humiliates someone else, such as an assistant, who played no role in the causal event.

I have also seen instances where the emotions of anger, hate, and rage can be totally out of proportion to the situations in which they are evoked. This might explain the extreme incident that I read about where one student accidentally bumped into another student in the corridor of their high school. The student who was bumped reacted instantly. He reached into his backpack, pulled out a 9mm gun, and shot the student who bumped into him.

When parents or significant others don't fill their children's *Heart-of-Hearts* with enough love, and when their children fail to develop a strong sense of emotional, psychological, and physical acceptance and positive feelings of belonging, these children will try to find other ways to satisfy these needs. For instance, one way to assuage their deep and gnawing sense of vulnerability may be to join a gang, which they think will supply them with the support and the sense of security and belonging they crave. By being members of groups, adolescents also get a sense of power, of control, of importance, and of being valued and respected—perceptions and feelings that they often never get at home.

So, the basic law of one's *Heart-of-Hearts* is that what goes into your *Heart-of-Hearts* comes out in one form or another. When love, respect, treasuring, and positive feelings and perceptions fill your *Heart-of-Hearts*, healthy and constructive feelings, decisions, and behaviors result. When negative and unhealthy feelings and perceptions fill it, unhealthy and destructive feelings, decisions, and behaviors result.

For example, my dad was lovingly nurtured by both of his parents until he was four years old. His father then left to join the army and, while fighting, contracted a blood disease and died. Even though my dad, for all intents and purposes, lost his father at the age of four, the fact that he was treasured and cherished until then (and loved by his mother throughout his childhood), made him feel valuable for the rest of his life. As a result, during the many trials and tribulations that he has faced over the past ninety-three years, my dad has always had a positive and constructive approach and has acted out self-enhancing *Strategies*.

My mom, on the other hand, had a mother who never loved her and cut her down in every way from the very beginning of her life. According to my mom, her mother always wanted a boy but was never able to conceive one. So she seemed to hate my mom for being a girl, and for the close and protected relationship that my mom developed with her father. My mom remembers being four years old and recognizing the hatred that her mother had for her. It was then that my mom chose not to emulate anything about her mother. Instead, she decided that she would emulate her father, who was much more of a nurturer.

My mom readily admits that her life, from the first moment onward, has been full of negative, initially self-protective strategies that evolved into self-destructive strategies. And, while she can do good things for me and for others, she has never felt good enough about herself to do enough good things for herself. As a sad result, she has never come close to fulfilling the considerable potential that she has in many areas. Although she has been aware of her problems for many years, she has never been fully able to break free of her past.

So, here we have two individuals: my dad, who was involuntarily abandoned by his father at the age of four (but loved for years thereafter by his mother until her death); and my mom, who was in a sense abandoned by her mother the moment she left the womb.

My dad is positively and constructively proactive in the way he lives his life. My mom is negatively reactive in the way she comprises hers. The differences lie in how these two individuals were, or weren't, loved, nurtured, and valued at the very beginning of their lives; how their *Heart-of-Hearts* were filled; and how these realities are reflected in their feelings about themselves, the *Strategies* that they've adopted, and the decisions that they've made.

We have all been exposed to a unique combination of healthy and unhealthy experiences, treatment, and values, and our *Heart-of-Hearts* have been filled accordingly with varying amounts of positive and negative feelings. For many of us, that fortuitous combination dictates what forms our decision-making *Strategies* will take, including what forms our defense mechanisms for dealing and coping with life's many challenges are.

We often rely on our *Strategies* blindly. This is a very dangerous *Strategy*. By understanding our *Strategies*, we can hopefully see the true positive value, or lack thereof, of each one of them. If we can indeed do this, we can then decide which *Strategies* we must keep, which we must discard, and which we must modify and rework.

But here's the crucial point: My life and my feelings about myself began to change radically when the following fortuitous event occurred. My mother fell and broke her thighbone, which resulted in my dad and I bonding athletically. Through athletics, I gained his approval, his respect, and his friendship. I also accomplished some very positive things on the athletic field that fueled me to lose weight. These experiences helped me to fill my *Heart-of-Hearts* with good feelings about myself, and to discover what I was capable of accomplishing. But you don't have to wait for accidents or random events to occur before you begin filling your *Heart-of-Hearts* with positives.

There's no reason why you can't, step-by-step, proactively begin each day by doing just one good, enhancing thing for yourself. The more constructive decisions that you make for yourself, the better you'll feel about who you are and your ability to take positive ownership of your life. This is the truest and most empowering form of self-help. Remember, with each constructive decision that you make, you are refilling your *Heart-of-Hearts* with positive feelings, and thereby building up your reservoir of high self-esteem and valid feelings of self-worth. These feelings, in turn, will motivate and propel you to make more and more self-enhancing and wise decisions. It's a domino effect—one naturally leads to another.

This is why making sure that your decision will positively effect your *Heart-of-Hearts* is so very important—it puts you on the constructive decision-making track.

Now, as part of our *Heart-of-Hearts* discussion, I'd like to share with you my final two *Crunch Time Strategies*. I believe that they are most appropriately presented here with *Step 5*, because they address how certain *Strategies* and actions can positively or negatively effect one's *Heart-of-Hearts*.

VALUING THE MEANS AS WELL AS THE ENDS

Your sense of self-worth, in large part, depends,
On the means you choose, to attain your ends.

I vividly remember a tennis tournament that I played in years ago. During one match, it appeared to most of the spectators that one of the players, Tom, called a number of his opponent's shots out when in fact they were in. After winning the match, Tom walked over to me and defensively confided: "Ya know, people think I cheated him. Screw it! Besides, I've learned that the only thing anyone cares about or remembers is who won the tournament, right? No one gives a damn how you win. They don't care if you were honest, tried hard, or were a good sport. It's all crap! All that counts in the rankings and to the team is the result."

Tom's assessment of what really counts is a sad—but often very true—commentary regarding our society's value system. As we've discussed, all too often we value and glorify the ends—the positive results that we achieve—but we almost never value, pay attention to, or examine the means by which we attain those results and successes.

For example, a local news manager once said to me that he has the ratings of his local newscasts broken down into three-minute segments. This way, he can compare one day's news ratings with the next, and specifically identify which particular stories resulted in a viewership increase or decrease. He does this by identifying at what points during a newscast viewers tuned in or out. With this information, he then decides which stories to continue to run in a later newscast, or the next day. For this television station and for many others, the defining data is not the importance of the story to the community that the station is serving, but which stories give them the highest ratings. The end is what counts, not the means (the content of the stories or how beneficial the information is to the viewers).

Why do tobacco companies do all they can to glorify smoking

through their advertisements and sponsorship of events? Why do the media and various events accept the tobacco companies' dollars? Why did people (before legislation was passed forbidding it) hand out free packs of cigarettes to children and teenagers on beaches and other public places? All of the people engaging in these acts knew that smoking kills, or at least is dangerous to one's health.

Why? Because the bottom line is all that we're taught and positively reinforced to care about. Our society has become obsessed with ends. Through various rationalizations and forms of repression, we sweep despicable and degrading means under our carpets. For many, the end of achieving financial or other success has become a great deodorant. It covers up the stench from the all-too prevalent philosophy of: "It *smells* (our means of goal attainment) but it *sells* (it achieves our desired end)."

The problem with being ends-oriented and paying little or no attention to the means of goal attainment is that even though our society only focuses on the ends, we, in our *Heart-of-Hearts*, can't truly hide our poor behavior from ourselves—because most of the time, in our *Heart-of-Hearts*, we know better! As a result, at the end of the day, our elaborate rationalizations and mental Band-Aids can't eradicate the severe damage that our poor behavior has done to our self-image and to our feelings of self-esteem (or lack thereof). They poison our *Heart-of-Hearts*.

I know many people like Tom, the tennis player, who deep down loathe themselves and feel less-than for deciding that it's necessary for them to cheat and take the lower means to attain their ends. I know that Tom's feeling of self-worth was so low that he felt that he needed to cheat in order to succeed. (One destructive decision leads to another.) As a result, when he played a really big match—with referees and lines-people—he'd almost always lose, because in his *Heart-of-Hearts*, he didn't feel that he had the real "goods" to win without cheating. As a result, more often than not, he collapsed at *Crunch Time*.

The preceding thoughts aren't meant to be "preachy." The fact is, your means of goal attainment can either make you feel worthy or worthless. If you don't respect yourself and feel that you are worthless or worth little, you won't make enhancing decisions for yourself and then implement them fully and successfully. Why? Because you have little or no positive self-esteem to propel you to make constructive decisions. Conversely, if you are buoyed by the valid feelings that you are indeed worthy and "worth it," these feelings will motivate you to make enhancing decisions now and throughout your life . . . and propel you to see them through in the long run.

Another story that reflects where our society is today was told to me years ago. It was a slow news day. Then, suddenly, word of the Oklahoma City bombing cut through the newsrooms like a knife through butter. One newsroom member allegedly blurted out, "Oh, God—but, thank God!"

In essence, what that reporter meant was, "Oh, God, too bad for the many people who lost their lives and their loved ones, and for those who will be permanently injured. But thank God we have a huge story. A tragedy! Just the kind of story that makes for great news and monster ratings. Breaking national stories are defining moments for individuals and news departments. Stars will be born. Maybe one of those stars will be *me*."

That reporter was sent to Oklahoma later that day by her station. Upon her arrival there, she camped out, hour after hour, at the home of a family that had just lost a loved one in the bombing. She remained there until she could "ambush" her prey. Eventually, she was able to interview the mother of one of the men who had died. Throughout the interview, she allegedly asked question after question, trying to dredge up every bit of pain, hurt, and heartache from the victim's mother. Upon her return to the newsroom, the reporter was allegedly thrilled to report to her news management and colleagues that, "I not only got the interview . . . but I made her [the victim's mother] *cry*! Wait 'til you see it [the videotape of the interview]. It's *great*!"

Unfortunately, this type of story isn't a new one for me. Time after time, I've witnessed broadcast and print reporters, in their efforts to create a story that's compelling or titillating, trample on people's legal and moral rights of privacy and their emotional well-being, and on sound journalistic principles as well. This is all done in search of the scoop, the ratings point, increased readership, the Emmy, the recognition, the piece of "tape," the story that will get the reporter his or her next (better) position, etc. All of these are worthwhile ends. The problem lies in the insensitive and/or inhumane means of their attainment.

As "Jerry Maguire"—the character played by Tom Cruise in the film of the same name—said as he was unceremoniously fired and kicked out of his sports-representation firm, "There's such a thing as manners . . . a way of treating people." In many ways, this chapter is all about "manners"—the *manner* in which you make your decisions and thereby conduct your life. How you feel about yourself is a direct outgrowth of how you conduct yourself (i.e., how you treat yourself and others), when aiming to attain your goals. One begets the other. *Therefore, it is of the utmost importance for you to craft decision-making Strategies that value the quality of your means of goal attainment* as much as—and, in some cases, even more than—the ends that you seek to attain. By doing this, you will feel good enough about yourself to make constructive decisions and do good things for yourself.

BEING SENSITIVE TO OTHERS: PUTTING YOURSELF IN ANOTHER'S SHOES

When I was about seven years old, my mom and I had a memorable food-shopping experience. Because it was Saturday, the store was crowded with customers and things were moving slowly, because there was only one checkout line. When we arrived at the register, the sixteen- or seventeen-year-old checker seemed frazzled. As she rang up our items as quickly as possible, I noticed that she didn't charge us for the half-gallon carton of milk. With a smile on my face, thinking something great had just happened, I quickly told my mom what I had just observed.

Ever so discreetly, my mom asked the checker whether she had rang up the milk. The checker quickly perused the cash-register tape and realized that she hadn't. She then thanked my mom profusely. She told us that she had been at the cash register for more than five hours without a break and could barely see straight. She also thanked my mom for calling the oversight to her attention in a way that didn't cause Mr. Jonowski, the store owner, to find out. (A very constructive and sensitive decision on my mom's part.)

When we got into the car, my mom turned to me and asked, "Kenny, why would you want to cheat the store owners out of money that they deserve? They work hard for their income. How would you like it if someone did that to you, or to me, or to Dad? Would that be right or fair? Put yourself in their place." Her words hit home. In my *Heart-of-Hearts*, I got it.

My mom continued, "And what about the cashier? She's working hard, on her day off from school, for very little money. What if Mr. Jonowski found out that she had made a mistake because she was tired? Would you want him to take the cost of the milk out of her salary? Or worse, what if Mr. Jonowski fired her for the mistake she made? Is that something you would want to be responsible for? What if she needs the job to help put herself through school? Or to help her parents? Or because she was saving up for something that's important to her?

"Kenny, my father and mother owned a grocery store just like the Jonowskis do, and we didn't make much money. So I understand how important it is to be paid for every item. *When making your decisions, try to put yourself in the shoes of those who will be affected by your decisions. Treat them as you'd like to be treated. Our capacity to be sensitive to others is what makes us human.*"

I'll never forget that day or that lesson. In my *Heart-of-Hearts*, I believe that being more sensitive to others—by treating them as I'd like to be treated—is the best way for me to grow into someone about whom I can feel good, and, at the same time, increase those wonderful feelings of high self-esteem and self-worth.

Striving to be sensitive to others when reaching your decisions is a very self-enhancing thing to do, because you will feel *good* about doing something positive or enhancing for someone else. By doing so, you will feel even better about who you are, which in turn will fuel you to make even more self-enhancing decisions . . . because once again you, in your *Heart-of-Hearts*, will feel that you're worth it!

Now let's review *Step 5* (Explore How Your Decision Will Affect Your *Heart-of-Hearts*) and study the implementation of this *Step* through two illustrations.

As discussed earlier, when Matt Lauer was the newsreader and fill-in host on the *Today* show, his popularity grew by leaps and bounds. As time passed, it became clear to many people at NBC that Matt would fit in better than Bryant Gumbel as the permanent host of *Today*. As a result, Matt and I were approached one day by an NBC news executive, who asked whether we would be interested in "quietly" negotiating a deal for Matt to replace his best friend, Bryant, while Bryant was still in the job.

When I discussed this proposed "secret" negotiation with Matt, he immediately responded by saying that he would have absolutely no part of any negotiation or discussion about replacing Bryant before Gumbel himself decided whether he wanted to remain as the *Today* show host and sign a new contract with NBC.

Obviously, in this instance, Matt had been given the chance to secure the one position that he truly coveted (as long as he entered into and successfully concluded the negotiation with NBC). However, Matt decided that this course of action didn't feel right to him, and it wasn't the way he chose to conduct his business.

Months later, Bryant decided on his own to leave NBC, and with Bryant's full support, Matt gracefully and seamlessly succeeded him. Recently, I asked Matt about the incident. In essence, he said that, "How we conducted ourselves made me feel good about my eventual ascension to hosting *Today*. Bryant is my closest friend, I couldn't do anything to undermine him. I feel even better about where I am [today] because we did it the right way."

"No, Matt," I countered, "*You* did it the right way! It was your decision to take the high road, and you deserve to feel great (in your

Heart-of-Hearts) about where you are, and even better, about *how* you got there."

In another illustration, during the past fifteen years that I've owned my own company, I have been approached by a number of other agencies asking whether I'd be interested in selling it. Only once, about seven years ago, did I give any serious consideration to the idea. Several positive values attracted me about that prospective buyer and situation:

- I liked and trusted the CEO of the company, who was a personal friend;

- I had fond memories of my experiences working at the William Morris Agency, because the company represented many of the world's top actors, writers, directors, singers, and rock groups, and the diversity of information that I acquired, and things that I experienced, were both intellectually stimulating and exciting. If I sold my company in this instance, I would once again be part of a major agency and could enjoy all of the positive experiences that it could provide;

- I would become part-owner of a major agency and a member of its board of directors. This kind of ownership position would provide me with a new, challenging, and, hopefully, a positive, stimulating situation;

- As part-owner of the agency, I would share in its profits, so if things went well, I would receive some very substantial year-end bonuses;

- Because the agency had a number of talented agents in its employ, I would have some very gifted agent-teammates to work with.

There were also several negative points about selling my company and merging with this potential buyer:

• My life as I knew it, and the freedom to do what I choose, when I choose, and how I choose—which comes with owning my company—would be gone. I would have to answer to many people;

• The yearly salary that was offered to me wasn't appreciably better than the salary I was currently making. Besides, I was ecstatic with the salary that I was already earning with my own company;

• The board members of the agency didn't look happy or healthy to me. They looked very stressed out. I, on the other hand, exercised every day, had no stomach problems or ulcers, and my hands didn't shake. I was physically and emotionally in good shape;

• Most important, my clients and staff members would have suffered significantly in their own ways if I sold the company. For example, in many instances, the potential buyer-agency charged a higher commission to their clients than we charged. I wouldn't think of passing that increase on to our clients, who had been good and loyal enough to follow me when I left William Morris. Loyalty, I believe, goes both ways.

Additionally, there would be loyal, long-term members of my wonderful staff who would not be needed by the major agency, because the agency already had people who performed the same functions that these staff-members perform for me. As a result, the buyer-agency would either let these members of my company go, or dramatically diminish their roles and salaries.

After weighing some of the pros and cons of the sale, I used *Step 5* to explore how my decision would affect my *Heart-of-Hearts*.

After some soul-searching, I concluded that I couldn't be disloyal to my clients or to my long-term staff members. I reasoned that people often try to wash away the stench of a hurtful decision by rationalizing that "business is business," but in my *Heart-of-Hearts*, I would know that if I hurt those who trusted me for years, worked hard with me and for my benefit, and who gave their valuable time and lives to be a positive part of mine. I would lack character and to my way of thinking, character counts when making decisions. I realized that my self-esteem and good feelings about myself would be greatly diminished if I didn't consider and appropriately value the security and futures of the individuals who had been there for me.

All of the power, money, and prestige of being part-owner of a major talent agency wouldn't justify a hurtful and harmful decision that would diminish and possibly poison my *Heart-of-Hearts* feelings of self-esteem and self-worth.

So for the benefit of my clients and my staff members, and for the well being of my *Heart-of-Hearts*, I made the self-enhancing and constructive decision not to sell.

I know in my *Heart-of-Hearts* that I made the right, soul-enhancing, and humane decision regarding the sale of my company, according to my unique value system . . . and because I did this, my *Heart-of-Hearts* is filled with good feelings. The staff members who know that I didn't sell them out appreciate me for it, and this makes me and my *Heart-of-Hearts* feel great . . . and that's what truly counts for me at the end of the day, and, I believe, will count for me at the end of my life.

I was truly constructive and considerate, and I let my character help guide me to my very self-enhancing decision.

However, please note that there may well be instances when it might be appropriate for me to sell my company. For example, a different proposal, at another time, might provide or allow for the creation of options that will give me a better opportunity to utilize and/or protect the services of my employees, and also keep our clients' commission structure intact. If this situation arises, the *Step 5* exploration into my *Heart-of-Hearts* could well lead me to make a completely different decision.

Once again, *Step 5* states that when reaching your decisions, explore and accurately assess how they will affect your *Heart-of-Hearts*. And remember that whether you have feelings of high or low self-esteem and self-worth depends upon the decisions that you make.

Step 6

FRAME YOUR DECISIONS, BY FINDING YOUR EMOTIONALLY-CHARGED TRIGGER

If decisions are your opportunities to take ownership of your life and make it better, then it is up to you to take full advantage of these opportunities. If you want to act in ways that will reflect your most cherished and important values and will lead to the fulfillment of your dreams and goals, great decisions are the vehicles that will take you where you want to go.

One of the keys to success is to put yourself in the best position possible to succeed. You can do this by *Framing* your decisions in such an emotionally-charged way as to significantly increase the chances that you will act in a manner that will help you to achieve your most cherished goals.

Earlier, we discussed my mom's prior problem of always being late, and the concept of communicating through emotionally *touching* someone. That is, crafting and communicating an idea or thought in a specific way so that the individual whom you are addressing can personally relate to it, understand it, be deeply touched and stirred by it (i.e., find the right personal trigger), and be compelled to take constructive action.

When I asked my mom why this particular communication so profoundly affected her that she, once and for all time, was able to take steps to rid herself of the destructive behavior of always being late, she replied, "Because I hated and absolutely abhorred being anything like my mother. The intensity of the feeling moved and compelled me to change. I then and there decided that I liked being nothing like my mother much more than I liked being able to take my time getting dressed, doing my hair, and looking beautiful. I overwhelmingly valued the payoff of being the opposite of her. There was absolutely no comparison."

The reason my mom changed from continually engaging in destructive and self-sabotaging decision-making and behavior when it came to her tardiness, to engaging in constructive and self-enhancing decision-making and behavior, lies in the fact that my dad's communication to my mom was so *emotionally charged* that it overcame and overrode the previously overpowering compulsion that led her to always be late. This is of monumental decision-making importance, because just as my dad was able to trigger and incite my mom to take positive action, through his emotionally-charged communication, *so too can you move, compel, incite and emotionally charge yourself—through effective framing of the issue before you—to counteract, override, and vitiate the negative emotions that lead you to make destructive and self-sabotaging decisions.*

For example, I know that there were certain strong emotions within me as a child that caused me to gorge myself on fattening foods whenever I had the opportunity. Not surprisingly, I became fat. However, things drastically changed when I said to myself, and *really meant* it, "I *hate* being fat and made fun of! I *hate* being romantically rejected by girls, because I'm fat and unattractive! I *hate* not being able to fit into the cool clothes that other kids wear! I *hate* being fat, slow, and clumsy on the paddle tennis court or on the school athletic field! I *absolutely hate* how I feel about myself. So when I'm offered fattening cookies, candy, or macaroni and cheese, I'll immediately think to myself, 'No! No more being laughed at, rejected, and feeling horrible about my weight! This part of my life is over!!!' I will be resolute about my decision to say, 'No, thank you,' every time I'm offered any fattening food, candy, dessert, or drink! My answer will be automatic."

By clarifying and identifying my most cherished values, by pushing my most sensitive and personal buttons, by clarifying my real values, and by building up an emotionally powerful charge, I was able to overcome the self-destructive emotions that had previously led me to act in a self-sabotaging manner.

The key to constructing the most effective and emotionally-charged "decision *Frame*," is to dig deep and honestly identify what emotion within you is so personally powerful that it will override and/or nullify any competing, destructive emotions, urges, temptations, or weaknesses, so that you are free to act in a constructive and self-enhancing manner congruent with your true constructive values.

We know that *Step 2* is to "State What The Issue Is." In *Step 6*, your goal is to *Frame* the decision. Let's be clear about the difference. We will use the term "state" to mean setting forth a clear, concise, objective recitation of the issue to be resolved. Conversely, *"Framing"* means crafting a very personal, emotionally-charged posturing of the issue. "Stating" the issue has no agenda attached to it. As you will see, *Framing* has a very definite agenda—to lead you to make a constructive and life-enhancing decision.

The following are some examples of "stating" the issue before you:

1) Should I have a slice of pumpkin pie?
2) Should I go to the movies this evening?
3) Should I stay late tonight and finish the project, or play cards?
4) Should I take some quiet time this weekend to catch up on things and gather my thoughts, or should I go to Las Vegas with my friends?
5) Should I forgo my vacation to stay in town and fill in for the main anchor?

OK. Now let's go back to *Framing* the issue before you.
Once you have weighed the relative importance of your values and

goals in a given situation, the means by which you can put yourself in the best position to make a great decision is to carefully craft, or *Frame*, your most logical, constructive, and self-enhancing choice in a manner that accurately reflects your most important values and *touches* you so personally that you are *triggered* and *compelled* to make the most life-enhancing decisions—and to continue making them.

For example, here are "decision *Frames*" that "*touch*" me.

1) Do I want to say, "No, thank you," to the mozzarella marinara that I'm being offered, or do I want to wind up in a hospital room being operated on for clogged arteries?

2) Do I want to risk blowing years of practice and sacrifice by going out to a party tonight, instead of going to bed early and being really ready for my very important tournament match tomorrow—a tournament that I would absolutely be elated to win, and would be devastated to lose if I knew that I didn't give it my all?

3) Do I really want to smoke cigarettes and get lung cancer and die a painful death? Do I want yellow teeth, distasteful cigarette breath, and clothes that reek from cigarette smoke? Do I also want to endanger people whom I care about with my secondhand smoke?

4) Do I want to have unprotected and random sexual relations, with the very real risk of AIDS and sexually transmitted diseases being so great? Do I want to be so self-destructive as to risk ruining my wonderful life—and possibly the lives of those who have relations with me—because of one thoughtless, lazy, selfish, and/or weak moment?

I *frame* these questions so that they push my buttons; so that they compel me to act with strength, resolve, and purpose. These "*Frames*" *touch* me, impact me, *trigger* me, drive me, and buoy me—for the moment, over time, and for all time. The images move me and *compel* me to stick with the constructive decisions I've made, and to continue to make them throughout my life.

Framing issues makes my choices clear, easy, and inevitable—because the *Framing* reflects my true values. More specifically.

1) I want to spend my life being healthy—not in some hospital operating room or intensive care unit. I'd rather be outside, on the tennis or paddle tennis court, or on the beach. I'll skip the clogged arteries. Forget the mozzarella marinara!

2) I want to win the tournament and reap the sweet fruits of the many seeds I've painstakingly sown. The partying can wait until after I've won (or lost). I'll opt to go to sleep early tonight.

3) I want to take positive ownership of my life and thereby enhance it—not write my death certificate. No smoking—no how, no way.

4) Being self-enhancing is a good thing. Being self-destructive by taking chances with my life isn't. I'll play it safe and hopefully never be sorry. Unprotected and random sex are out.

By *Framing* issues, I'm loading the dice in my favor. I'm allowing my most dearly held and clearly constructive values to be the magnet and my guide to *triggering* and motivating me to make the most self-enhancing decisions I'm capable of. *Framing* choices, as I have above, has put me in the best position possible to attain my goals and fulfill my most cherished dreams. Remember:

"Framing can put you in the best position
To make your most constructive decision."

If you *Frame* your choices correctly and compellingly, and then decide accordingly, you can then claim the victories (both psychological and material) and the wonderful and empowering feelings of high self-esteem that come with doing something constructive for yourself.

Other examples of *framing* that *touch* or *trigger* might be:

- Do I want to keep smoking and risk not being around to see my children or grandchildren grow up?

- Do I want to focus so much on my work that one day I realize that the most vital and physically healthy years of my life have been lost to me forever?"

- Do I want to continue to ignore symptoms that I have by not seeing a doctor, and take the chance that these things have progressed too far to be cured? How will I feel if I learn that an early trip to the doctor would have in all likelihood resulted in my full recovery?

The key to making great decisions is crafting the most value-reflecting and emotionally-charged *Frames* possible.

Effectively *Frame* your decisions. Then claim your victories, your life, your goals, and *your dreams*.

One last thing to remember: As your most cherished values change, your *Frames* may also change. So if, God forbid, someone's only grandchild died, the *Frame* of, "Do I want to keep smoking and take the risk of not being around to see my grandchild grow up?" would obviously no longer be compelling. In this instance, the decision-maker would once again have to search deep into his or her *Heart-of-Hearts* to find another emotionally charged, *touching*, and/or *triggering* value and reason for her to forgo smoking, and then fashion the *Frame* accordingly.

Step 7

MAKE A GREAT,
LIFE-ENHANCING
DECISION

Step 8

CELEBRATE AND SAVOR YOUR CONSTRUCTIVE DECISIONS, AND EVALUATE YOUR DECISION-MAKING STRATEGIES

TRUE POST-*CRUNCH TIME* DECISION MAKING

Many people in life are great starters, but few have the "internal goods" to be great *finishers*.

In the music industry, there have been hundreds and hundreds of musicians who recorded one hit song and were never heard from again—the infamous "one-hit wonders." On the other hand, artists such as Elton John, Paul McCartney, and Madonna release hit after hit, year after year, and remain popular to this day.

One of the skills that all of the above mentioned artists have in common is that they write much or all of their own music. They understand their craft, and they've mastered the inner formulas (and *Strategies*) that have enabled them to continue to adapt their performances to the times, and thereby remain successful over time. These extraordinarily successful individuals have the internal skills to determine their own fate over the long run, unlike many of the one-hit wonders whose fate rested upon whomever they could find to write their next song.

Another example comes to mind of some excellent strategy re-working that allowed a very adaptable decision-maker to flourish in the long run. Years ago, I listened to a basketball game between the Chicago Bulls and the Los Angeles Lakers. Throughout the first three quarters of the game, the Lakers dominated the NBA Champion Bulls and their superstar, Michael Jordan. The Lakers led by more than twenty points as the fourth quarter began. However, by the end of the game, Jordan and his teammates had insightfully and effectively modified their strategies, and then implemented them. They thereby elevated their quality of play enough to eke out a stunning victory. Just a few weeks later, Jordan and the NBA East All-Stars also fell behind by more than twenty points to the West team in the NBA All-Star game. Once again, Jordan led a comeback that resulted in a victory.

There is no coincidence here. Unquestionably, Michael Jordan is an incredibly gifted athlete. But in both of the games mentioned above, he was playing against other incredibly gifted athletes. The huge difference is Michael Jordan has the ability to stick with *Strategies* that are enhancing, as well as the ability to modify or discard others that aren't. He is flexible, and this quality makes a huge difference in the growth and enhancement of his performance over time. As a result, he is an unparalleled finisher.

We have all known individuals who decide to make resolutions, especially at reflective times such as New Year's, only to abandon them shortly thereafter. We have all seen people decide to go on diets, lose large amounts of weight, and then gain it all back. *But the greatest diet books and formulas must also be accompanied by constructive psychological and emotional Strategies—otherwise, in the long run, failure is inevitable.*

It is your goal to not only develop the internal goods that will enable you to make great decisions, but to also maintain and enhance what you've built over time. Like Madonna and Elton John, you want to make hit after decision-making hit *throughout your lifetime.*

Step 8 is devoted to your post–*Crunch Time* thinking and behavior. That is, how you think and act *after* you have made a good or a weak decision, so that you can "stay the course" and/or improve upon it—in the case of a good decision—or modify or completely change your course if the original decision that you reached wasn't the healthiest, most efficacious one possible.

We began our journey together by discussing the importance of laying a strong inner foundation for ourselves. This foundation is made up of the *Eight Steps* as well *Crunch Time Strategies* and *Strata-Gems* delineated in this book, along with any other new or reworked healthy and constructive *Strategies* that you have concluded will help you to make life-enhancing decisions and live your life in a positive and wise manner.

Let's assume that you indeed have made a constructive decision, and that you have also acted consistently with it. For instance, you have decided to no longer reflexively react to situations, but instead, you now take time to step back and craft responses that reflect your heartfelt and highest values. You have successfully implemented this *Strategy* for several days, with great results. The next steps to take are to (1) internally acknowledge what you've accomplished, (2) explore and understand the ramifications of your new *Strategy*, and (3) experience, celebrate, and enjoy your success. Revel in it!

Acknowledging your healthy decisions and actions makes you pay internal attention to them and take positive note of them. Focusing on good things—done well—plays a significant role in developing your knowledge and feelings of mastery and competence, and your ability to indeed take proactive ownership of your life. This in turn can lead to the birth and the evolution of the all-important feelings of earned and valid self-esteem.

Exploring, understanding, and cerebrally and emotionally celebrating your healthy decisions will help instill them in your memory bank, and will later remind you of how you reached your decisions and why you chose the courses of action that you did. By understanding these things, you will thereafter be able to reason for yourself when, where, and why similar decisions and acts may or may not be appropriate and constructive in certain future situations.

If you're armed with these sound understanding and reasoning skills—unlike the one-hit wonders—you'll have put yourself in the very best position possible to have decision-making success after success—

because you'll have the internal goods to produce them yourself. Hopefully, in time, even reflexively.

Being able to understand and successfully reason through tough decisions, choices, and conflicts can once again give you the gratifying and empowering feelings of mastery and ownership, which will also enhance your feelings of self-esteem.

Enjoying your successes helps to positively reinforce healthy decisions and behaviors for the future. We *like* doing things that make us feel good. Giving yourself valid and deserved internal credit when you do good things for yourself or for others is in itself a very gratifying act and a wise decision. It makes you feel good about you, and it will compel you to do good things for yourself and for others, again and again.

My clients have told me that there are few things as exhilarating and gratifying as "nailing" a good live report or a great interview. The feelings of accomplishment and ownership are huge. And it is those acknowledged and good feelings that often propel them to attempt, and often master, more and greater things in the future. *It inspires them to take chances and to grow!*

I do my best to contribute to this positive and constructive process. When one of my clients does something well on the air, I point out the specific elements of the report that I liked, and I articulate why I liked them and why they worked for me. By being compliment-specific, I believe that the praise and the reasoning behind the comments will more effectively click into my client's *Heart-of-Hearts* and memory banks, so that the specific strategy for behavior that I complimented will be more apt to become part of their journalistic repertoire. Additionally, by being specific, I am more effectively increasing my client's valid feelings of self-esteem.

There are also times when general compliments are appropriate. For example, the other day, one of my clients was offered a huge network position, which he couldn't accept because the change of location would be too detrimental to his family's stability. After he turned the job down, I took the opportunity to call and remind him that he should take a moment to appreciate how very far he had come in his career. The proof of his growth was indisputable, as one of the most prestigious network news operations chose him for the position over everyone else in the country. I wanted him to see and feel his talent and success through this tangible reality test.

Just as I help my clients grow with honest critiquing, you must be a teacher, coach, and counselor for yourself. When you do something well, internally acknowledge it, understand how and why it was done well, and integrate it into your collection of constructive *Strategies*.

As you master your decision-making processes and thereby do good things for yourself and for others, take time to enjoy and applaud your successes. As a result, the valid and earned self-esteem that fills your *Heart-of-Hearts* will increase and be reinforced. And when your *Heart-of-Hearts* is full with enough of these positive feelings regarding your ability to master tasks and enhance yourself, these feelings of self-esteem will lead to valid feelings of self-love. It is these reinforced, empowering feelings that will anchor you in times of indecision, conflict, or crisis, and catalyze you to do good things for yourself and others.

Throughout my career, I have advised my clients to take care of and cherish their emotional and physical well-being, because without them, my clients aren't much good to themselves, their employers, or those whom they care about. As Stephen Covey writes in his highly acclaimed book *Seven Habits of Highly Effective People*, "If you don't take care of the Golden Goose, there won't be any eggs for anyone." In this instance, practicing self-love is not acting selfishly. On the contrary, it is a valuing and reinforcing of the physical, intellectual, and emotional gifts that have been bestowed upon you so that you consciously choose, time after time, to make healthy decisions that will preserve and enhance those gifts.

Once your *Heart-of-Hearts* is filled with enough self-esteem and self-love, you can then feel good and loving enough to do good things for others (without an ulterior motive). The airlines advise parents and caregivers to put their oxygen masks on first, before putting them on a child. This way, once the parent or caregiver is "equipped," he or she is then better able to help the child. Similarly, if you can fill your memory banks with enough healthy decision-making *Strategies*—which in turn will produce significant feelings of valid self-esteem and self-love within you—you will be much more emotionally equipped to then take care of and enhance others. And lifting others will continue to increase your feelings of self-esteem and self-love.

Additionally, when true self-love fills your *Heart-of-Hearts*, this positive energy can propel you to make the effort to reach healthy and enhancing decisions and to follow through with them over time—because you honestly feel that you're worth it!

This formula has worked for me and for many others. Therefore, the key is for you to refill your memory bank with the *Crunch Time Strategies* and other healthy and enhancing strategies for behavior that you've created or adopted, so that they are etched in your mind and are instilled within you for the rest of your life. This will result in your making great decisions over time. You can accomplish this in the following way: After each good or weak decision that you make, review, evaluate, and learn whatever you can. *Remember that mistakes remain mistakes only if you don't learn from them*. Instill each lesson into your memory through the process of internal articulation, visualization, analysis, and understanding of the positive or negative results of your decisions. When this has been done, follow the *Strategy* of retaining your healthy and enhancing *Strategies* and modifying or discarding your unhealthy or diminishing ones.

Here's an example of applying the components of *Step 8*. A few months ago, I was driving in an underground parking lot at about 8:00 A.M. on a weekend morning. As I expected, there were only a few cars in the huge lot at that time. Upon approaching the intersection, I couldn't see if there were any cars coming from the left, because there was a concrete wall blocking my view. Figuring that there'd be no one driving up to the intersection at that time, I unconsciously made a "rolling stop" through the intersection without looking to my left. As I was halfway through, a driver on the left, whose vision had also been blocked by the wall, also failed to stop at the stop sign. She hit my car on the back fender. Luckily, we were both going slowly, so neither of us was hurt, and there was minimal damage to our cars.

However, after this experience, I took the time to examine and understand what had happened. I acknowledged that I had made a bad decision by not coming to a total stop in order to see if there were any cars about to cross or turn into the intersection. The time of day, obviously, should not have played any role in my decision. I should always stop. I understood that in this instance I had escaped relatively unscathed, with some minor car damage. I made sure that I realized that I could have been seriously injured and that I could have seriously injured someone else. I visualized both of these horrible possibilities and made sure that they were vividly etched into my memory.

I then reworked my driving *Strategy*. I vowed that from that day on, I would always come to a full stop and survey all approaching cars, no matter what the time of day or how populated the area. Because I dearly value my health and the health of others, I made sure that this new *Strategy* emotionally and cognitively clicked within me.

Ominously, about two months later, in the same parking lot, I approached the same blind intersection. This time I made a full stop before moving forward. In what seemed like an instant after I stopped, and before I could survey the traffic, a car raced through the stop sign and the intersection. Had I made a rolling stop, as I had before, the driver's side of my car and I would've been smashed to smithereens. I could have been killed or certainly seriously injured. No question about it.

After the car sped by, I took a few moments to realize and mentally imprint what had just happened and what could have occurred if I hadn't constructively modified my stop-sign *Strategy*. I made sure that the significance of the experience and its positive outcome, due to my new constructive *Strategy*, were clearly instilled within me—for the long run.

In effect, I was reinforcing the same *Strategy* modification formula that I used earlier in my life to lose weight—once I discerned that my true unconflicted value was to "be thin," my dieting decisions began more and more to reflect this value. For instance, before and during the times that I made decisions to eat nonfattening foods I visualized and dwelled on all the positive things that would result if I practiced disciplined eating. After I made each of these constructive decisions, I acknowledged what I had done and internally applauded my discipline, my decision, and my behavior. As I began to lose weight and other positive things began to happen to me, I jubilantly took note of the positive, tangible results. I enjoyed them and was exhilarated by them. I'd look in the mirror and etch into my memory, the reflection of the leaner, fitter me. I loved it! I began to fit into clothes that I had always wished I could wear. As I became more agile and successful athletically, I made sure that I fully acknowledged and understood that the successes and pleasures that I was enjoying and experiencing were the direct and very tangible result of my new weight-loss *Strategy*. And I did it all myself!

This successful mastery led to my developing within me some very legitimate and earned feelings of self-esteem. And it was this reservoir of good feeling that led to feelings and behavior that reflected real self-love. And it was my feelings of self-love and wanting to do good things for myself—along with the feelings that I deserved those good things and that I could, in fact, attain them—that have enabled me to keep my weight off for the past forty years. In fact, my decisions to refuse fattening foods have now become reflexive—I no longer even think about going off my diet. I am as sure as I can be—and I believe that those individuals who know me would agree—that I'll never be overweight again. My successful decision-making *Strategies* and my now-solid feelings of self-love will ensure it.

Once again, *Step 8* is to review, evaluate, keep, and/or modify and improve your constructive and self-enhancing *Strategies*, and to discard the weak, destructive, and diminishing ones. Then instill the enhancing *Strategies* into your memory bank, so that you can continue to make great decision after great decision—for the rest of your life!

A CLOSING NOTE

You now have the foundation, as well as the *Crunch Time Strategies,* the *Strata-Gems,* and the *Eight Crunch Time Steps,* for making constructive, efficacious, and life-enhancing decisions. You also have the ability and power to change your life for the better—starting right now! With each and every minor and major decision that you make!

It's time to take ownership of your life and to actively live it, in the most positive, constructive, and self-empowering way.

Carpe diem!